MUSIC AS YOGA

DISCOVER THE HEALING POWER OF SOUND

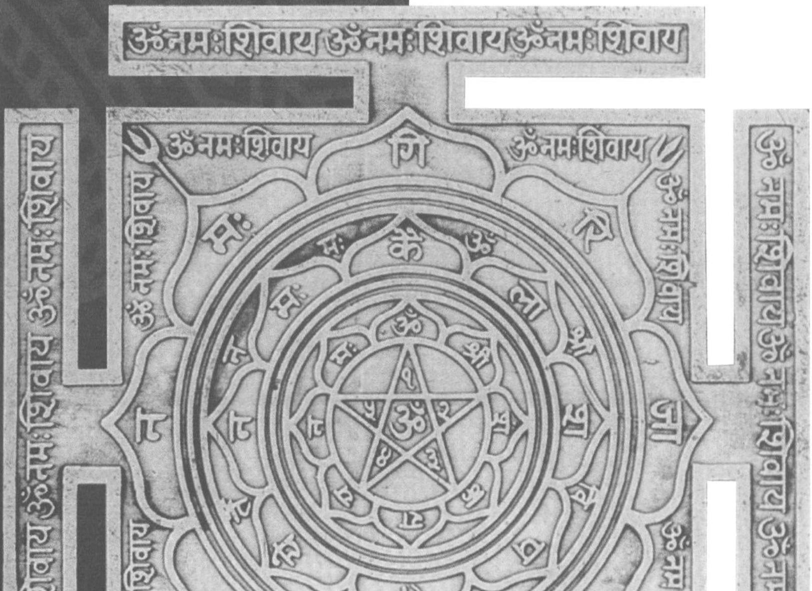
ॐ नमः शिवाय ॐ नमः शिवाय ॐ नमः शिवाय

MUSIC AS YOGA

DISCOVER THE HEALING POWER OF SOUND

PATRICK BERNARD

MANDALA
PUBLISHING

San Rafael

MANDALA
PUBLISHING

17 Paul Drive
San Rafael, CA 94903
Tel: 415.526.1380
Fax: 415.532.3281
Orders: 800.688.2218
E-mail: info@mandala.org
Website: www.mandala.org

Originally published in French as
Les secrets de la musique de l'âme
©1991 Imagine Records & Publishing

Designed by Insight Design
Printed in China through
Palace Press International

10 9 8 7 6 5 4 3 2 1

Library of Congress Cataloging-in-Publication
data available

ISBN 1-932771-00-X

CONTENTS

Illustrations

Cover photo by Michelangelo Durazzo. Yantra designs from
Mantras, Yantras & Fabulous Gems by Howard Beckman,
©Balaji Publishing Co., www.planetaryjewels.com

A sincere effort has been made to identify copyright holders and to seek their permission for the illustrations that appear in this work. Unintended omissions may have occurred due to the use of ancient or traditional art of questionable origin, or where research proved inconclusive. For questions concerning copyright or licensing, please contact the publisher at the address provided.

Preface

As citizens in a new age of mass communication, we are constantly subjected to the sonic abuse of the world's discordant noises. Unable to reside in a natural setting, many of us endure an around-the-clock assault upon the senses. Grinding gears, screeching brakes, blaring sirens, ringing cell phones and other modern trappings gradually weaken our bodies and minds. What's more, popular culture's idea of music often reflects the unconscious echo of the disruptive mechanisms that surround us. As we embark upon a new century, raucous vibrations, distortions and shrieks all too often replace the melodies of music.

In addition to this barrage of noise, even the spoken word is no longer sacred; more often it is used to achieve negative ends. To what extent can the cumulative effect of these noises and statements, often saturated by nihilism and negativity, devastate the inner sanctuary of our being? How many illnesses, disorders, maladjustments and suicides do these sounds provoke?

Contemporary composers share the responsibility of developing a type of music that can help heal the wounds inflicted by noise pollution, which has become the plague of modern times. More than simply relaxing music, new musical creations should compose sounds of transformation. Transforming anxiety into tranquil-

ity, fear and anguish into bounty and trust, ignorance into consciousness, pain into serenity—this should be the fundamental intention behind these creations. The source of inspiration and choice of sounds should fill listeners with a sense of completeness. This feeling is not imposed from the outside, but arises from a source within, an ever-present eternal energy, available to us all whenever we choose to turn within and connect to it, as the music of transformation helps us to do.

Furthermore, the energies of this type of music can carry attentive listeners to a supernatural atmosphere, which is peaceful, happy and anointed with the balm of unconditional love. This dimension, while unperceivable to the eye and ear, is accessible through contemplation of sacred texts and through intuition or transpersonal experience.

Here, everything is possible: everyday stress disappears, worries and tensions evaporate and you as a listener penetrate into the sphere of your own serenity. In that sphere, all your senses are captivated by a unique pleasure that is actually coming from within you. At this point, the keys of the universe are in your hands. You need only leave the doors of your heart and mind wide open for harmony to offer you the opportunity to rediscover your natural state, allowing you to return to who you really are.

acknowledgments

I would like first and foremost to acknowledge my life-partner, Anuradha Dauphinais, for her help, ever-present service attitude, love and devotion. I would also like to thank my publisher, Raoul Goff, who has been unfailingly encouraging, literally giving a new life to this book. To Lisa Fitzpatrick, I extend gratitude for her sincere support.

I am also truly indebted to N.D. Koster and Stephanie Marohn for their exceptional editorial assistance. Thank you to the Insight Design team for their creative input and expertise, especially Ian Szymkowiak.

I am thankful also to Buffy Williams at BlueSky Yoga Center in Florida, for using my music on a daily basis during her practice. I offer a collective prayer of thanks to all practitioners, yoga teachers, sound healers, healthcare personnel, massage therapists and all the listeners who have for the past 15 years sent numerous letters with touching stories related to the healing effects of my musical investigations. There are more people to thank for the development of this book than I can possibly name.

Finally, I would also like to thank my spiritual teacher, Swami B. R. Sridhar, who has facilitated the harmonization of everything in my life.

THE EFFECT OF SOUND VIBRATIONS

A JOURNEY ON UNCHARTED WATERS

Knowledge of the therapeutic nature of music stretches back to antiquity. Music was used to purify consciousness, with the understanding that illness only attacks where it finds weakness and that, more often than not, weakness stems from lack of balance or impurity in the body, mind or spirit. The saying, "In purity is strength" remains a basic truth.

To foster this kind of fortifying purity, the composer, and the listener, must develop an art that is in harmony with the laws of nature and truly values life. In the absence of such an art of living, one only creates confusion, disharmony and chaos.

As the science of sound becomes better known throughout the Western world, we will become aware of the countless influences that all the aspects of our being—body, mind and spirit—currently endure as we subject ourselves, either voluntarily or involuntarily, to staggering quantities of noises, sounds, rhythms and all kinds of melodies, the effects of which most of us do not presently realize.

As just one example, radio today has taken such a place in our lives that the listener is subjected to any and all sorts of musical material, anywhere, at any given time. There exists a global unconsciousness regarding the indelible effects of sound on the subtle elements of consciousness and memory. Like everything else in the universe, in and of itself radio is neither good nor bad. The way we use it determines the nature of the effects it has on us as a whole.

Music historian Cyril Scott's renowned book *Music: Its Secret Influence Through the Ages* demonstrates that the greatest of prudence should guide our actions in this area. In his work, originally published in 1933, Scott analyzes in detail music's effects on the mind and on the world of emotions. He shows us, for example, to what extent Handel's music influenced the Victorian era, how "his solemn and reverential music awakened in people of certain temperaments a marked feeling of exaggerated seriousness, expressed through a morbid inclination for funereal decors," and how "this was the result of a misconception of religion and of spiritual life in general."[1] He also explains how Beethoven was both a psychologist and a musician, and how his musical style has a powerfully liberating effect on the subconscious of those who listen to his music.

> There exists a global unconsciousness regarding the indelible effects of sound on the subtle elements of consciousness and memory.

Sounds do, in fact, act as stimuli that generate a thought process and liberate the energies stored in the subconscious. This gives us cause for concern in today's world, where particularly aggressive types of music exist. Just as Handel's musical vibrations influenced his epoch and Beethoven's symphonies have a liberating effect on listeners' minds, the violently destructive vibrations of certain syncopated rhythms create subconscious reflexes that vibrate through the phenomenon of resonance and are attuned to emotions associated with violence and destruction.

It is humanity's duty to initiate serious studies focusing on this topic to inform those unfortunate victims who cannot find in this type of music anything but what it proposes: frustration, pain, anxiety and destruction. Each musical vibration binds us to its corresponding level of existence. To be aware of this reality enables us to consciously choose the specific association that corresponds to our desires.

Some musical pieces are harmful, while others have calming and regenerating effects. Some forms of music overexcite then deplete, while others stimulate without enervating. According to Cyril Scott, the gluttonous character of syncopated rhythm deliberately rejects all spiritual and elevating content, producing instead an overstimulation of the nervous system and a subsequent weakening of the powers of concentration and self-control. In the light of this information, we should reexamine our conclusions about the alarmingly high suicide, depression and dropout rates in our culture.

THE ANCIENT WAY

Music, as the ancients knew, is a balm that soothes the heart. Through the power of suggestion, certain rhythms and melodies offer an antidote for human passions. Pythagoras deemed it possible for this suggestive power to contribute significantly to good health, provided it was used appropriately.[2] He termed

 this healing process "purification." He was the first to create a school to study the affect of rhythm on human passions, which he termed the "music of the spheres." He believed that the heavenly bodies in the sky were intrinsically linked to the sounds humans could make on plucked strings, and that there was profound healing to be found in the knowledge of that soothing music.

For his students, Pythagoras developed and adapted what are referred to as apparatus or devices, which are divinely created mixtures of certain diatonic, chromatic or enharmonic melodies. Through these, he postulated, it was easy to transfer or redirect the soul's passions—sadness, anger, pity, craving, pride, sloth and vehemence—provided they had taken shape recently or in secret. He righted each passion according to the rules of virtue, tempering them with appropriate melodies, which could be likened to beneficial medicines. Each night when his students went to sleep, Pythagoras performed specific odes and songs to rid them of diurnal disruptions and turmoil. Purifying their intellect of the fluctuations of bodily nature, he thus ensured for them a calm night's sleep with pleasant, sometimes even prophetic, dreams. When they awoke, he sang or played on his lyre other songs and appropriate modulations to free them of the sluggishness brought on by the night. Thus it is possible, according to Pythagoras, to purify the body and the mind using musical energies.

Trust in the transformative power of sounds was

also widespread in ancient China, where musical science was a part of the nobles' education. In Zen master Su Ma T'sien's historic memoirs, which date back to the first century B.C., we discover that certain notes have a beneficial manner on human conduct. T'sien wrote: "Sounds and music agitate and animate the arteries and the veins. This generates life-giving breath and brings to the heart harmony and rectitude. The *kong* note affects the spleen and brings saintliness to man. The *kio* note affects the liver and brings the harmony of perfect goodness to man. The *tche* note affects the heart and brings the harmony of perfect rites to man. The *yu* note affects the kidneys and brings the harmony of perfect wisdom to man."[3]

This manuscript makes it clear that healing physical disorders through sound vibration was common in ancient China. Moreover, the Su Ma T'sien manuscript demonstrates that the Chinese believed that all musical notes spring from the heart. The ancient manuscript ex-

plains that the sentiment, born of inner excitement, manifests in the exterior world in sound. When the sounds are beautiful, they are what we call musical notes. Hence (and this is where the message takes on its fullest meaning), the notes of a troubled period are those of hatred and irritation. The musical notes of a country falling into ruin are sad and worrisome and weigh on its people. Sounds and notes reflect the leadership of the time. Analyze the music of a people, of a nation, of a race and you will have a clear idea of the motivations, desires and priorities of its individuals. The music people listen to speaks volumes about who they are.

Numerous historical accounts tell us that noble-hearted kings regulated ancient Chinese music. These leaders were aware of the immense influence of musical vibrations on people's behavior. They knew that an unregulated way of life leads a society to disaster. Consequently, ritualistic art, dance, painting and especially music were regulated to a certain extent, thus establishing moderating principles for humankind. Music was never violent, so as not to provoke violence. It was not sad, so as not to draw listeners into a depressed state of mind. It did not concentrate on feelings of anger and fear, so as not to encourage anxiety among the masses.

> Sounds do, in fact, act as stimuli that generate a thought process and liberate the energies stored in the subconscious.

Humankind is compelled by an infinite number of sights, sounds and feelings. When people's affection and hatred have no governing rules of expression, they will be transformed upon being confronted with the stimuli for those emotions. The compassionate nature within individuals will be suppressed and they will be ruled primarily by their passions.

In ancient China, music unified the body, the heart and the mind. As is too often the case today—as anarchy rules how music is used—it divides rather than unifies. This dispersion of the physical, emotional and mental bodies leads to serious imbalances, which in turn cause severe sociological problems. Composers are in a position to create music that unites feelings and produces calming effects. They can help us rediscover our true spiritual identity and prevent the extinction of the heavenly principle in our societies. Music can better the heart. It serves to teach because it has the power to move us profoundly and because it brings change to customs and habits.

The ancient Chinese kings knew this, and, consequently, ensured that music was consistent in measure and harmony. This is not to say, as some will undoubtedly be quick to claim, that a somber and austere atmosphere prevailed. Music produces joy. But pleasure manifested in the absence of a harmonious art of living brings forth disorder. Sensual pleasure, for instance, when it knows no limits, when it is not controlled by consciousness, can produce cellular, and even terminal, maladies. According to the U.S. Department of Health and Human Services, for example, elevated dopamine levels in the brain can cause cellular disorders and incurable illness.[4] This is why ancient China established a rule, an art of living, and decreed that sounds be sufficient to create pleasure, but not to the point of negligence. Those who created music did so with the objective of attaining a moderated joy.

The goal of composers concerned with the inner workings of humankind and the expansion of its consciousness has always been to counter excesses. Working toward moderation, self-mastery, gentleness and expanded horizons is always better accomplished in simplicity.

SOUND IN THE AGE OF TECHNOLOGY

Most of the time we do not listen to music, we hear it. Few people have the ability to listen because listening is the gift of one's self to others. But what happens when we hear music? It has an effect on us, beneficial or otherwise. It can stimulate us or make us drowsy. Even if it is background music, to which we pay little attention, it works insidiously on our nervous system.

Imagine, for example, walking into a store. Music pours from loudspeakers, but we don't really listen to it. We go straight to the department that interests us, ignoring the background music. But the music is aware of us. It is interested in us. It cunningly penetrates into our bodies by way of what scientist Thomas Zébério calls "vortex-ring interstices," or the electromagnetic centers of the body.[5] Through these centers, music spreads and fulfills its mission: breaking down our defense mechanisms and encouraging us to buy products we don't really need. Our discernment is distracted and we are soon filling our bags with all kinds of unnecessary purchases. Such is the function of music as a marketing tool.

In pediatric psychologist Rolando Benenzon's book on music therapy, *Manual of Musicotherapy,* we find an account of the experience of the Italian physiologist Patria, who conducted historical experiments that determined the effect of certain sound combinations on the blood's circulation to the brain.[6] Among other forms of music, he used military marches such as the "Marseillaise" and was able to ascertain that blood circulation to the brain increased when the subject listened to military-type music.

Whether it is being used for marketing or military purposes, quite obviously music acts upon our cellular system as a whole. As Ralph Tegtmeier remarks in his *Guide to New Music for the Inner Journey:* "We do not generally try to entertain a perfectly conscious relationship with music. It is for us a source of liberation, often perhaps the only liberation we really know, and for this very reason we overestimate it. Once we reach this point, we become incapable of mistrusting it and are unable to protect ourselves effectively from the abusive influence it can have."[7]

In his informative work, *Your Body Doesn't Lie,* Dr. John Diamond shares the fruit of his research—discoveries that corroborate those of numerous other researchers—on music's effects on plants and on the human body. He had the idea of measuring the muscular reaction of patients listening to various types of music. He reports on his experiments as follows:

> Using hundreds of subjects, I found that listening to rock music frequently causes all the muscles in the body to go limp. The normal pressure required to control a strong deltoid muscle (a triangular muscle in the shoulder, used to lift the arm) in an adult male is approximately 40 to 45 pounds. When rock music is played, only 10 to 15 pounds of pressure is needed. Every major muscle of the body is linked to an organ. This means that a large proportion of the popular music to which we are exposed each day affects all the organs of our body. If we add up the hours of radio play throughout the world, we can see how enormous a

problem this is. The abnormal rhythm of rock music's beat (an anapestic rhythm—da-da-Da) and the music's high noise level induce weakness in us. Harmful music decreases physical energy, regardless of the volume at which it is listened to.[8]

Other clinical research has shown that, with an anapestic rhythm, the entire body is plunged into a kind of state of alert. This state provokes hyperactivity, anxiety, irritability, constant agitation and a decrease in the attention span. It becomes difficult to make decisions and the feeling that things are not going the way they should settles in. Then follows a loss of energy with no apparent cause.

In *The Healing Energies of Music,* author Hal A. Lingerman writes: "Destructive music causes damage not only to your physical body, but also to your emotions and mental processes. Such sounds affect your entire aura, making you feel psychically torn apart, fragmented, frightened, combative, isolated, tense and aimless. Such stressful, ugly sounds will also scatter your plans, and they will fog and frustrate your goals. Most tragically, discordant music will alienate you from your inner center of guidance, cutting you off from your conscious union with the Creator, leaving you feeling abandoned, and exposing you to being controlled by negative vibrations."[9]

There is an alternative, a life-enhancing way to cope with the modern world, and that is to remain constantly aware of the musical energies that surround us, pene-

> We are compelled to suspect that the vast majority of sounds produced in our modern world—whether described as musical or not—result in alarming functional disturbances in both adults and children.

trate our systems, exercise their suggestive powers on us and thus make us subject to their influence. This process is a state of vigilance, with nothing less than the human body and the heart at stake. Here the word heart refers to the subtle heart *chakra* situated a little behind the physical heart. It is in this tiny organic computer where music's emotional and sensory forces are processed. It is often necessary to be vigilant in order to protect oneself from, or conversely to take advantage of the beneficial effects of, musical energies and the many types of sounds that saturate our current environment.

Rolando Benenzon asks: "With the incredible development of sound in our current civilization, what changes have been brought about in enzyme-based mechanisms? We have no clear idea yet, but in all likelihood, these changes do not bode well for the future."[10]

We are compelled to suspect that the vast majority of sounds produced in our modern world—whether described as musical or not—result in alarming functional disturbances in both adults and children. These sounds can be unhesitatingly categorized as harmful to human well-being and detrimental to our evolution. But are we conscious of the effects of sounds on our being? Trustingly, yearround, we absorb all sorts of rhythms, tunes, melodies and harmonies, which are repeated *ad infinitum.* How many of us realize that the same music played again and again over a long period of time produces emotions that make a deep impression in our personalities, thus influencing the course of our lives?

Before contemplating music's effect on our soul, however, let us ask ourselves to what extent sounds influence our physical body.

WHen music Deafens

The obvious place to start in considering the physical effects of sound is the ear. The ear comprises three parts. The *outer ear* (auricle and auditory duct) collects sounds from the environment, which then magnify in the *middle ear* through the eardrum (a membrane) and the three tiny bones that are joined to one another. Vibrations next reach the *inner ear,* the cochlea, which sends a message to the brain through the auditory nerve. The deterioration of one of the parts of this extraordinary acoustic device results in hearing impairment. The lasting sensation of deafness and whistling in the ears that one feels when leaving a loud musical concert or nightclub are signs of cellular disorders of the auditory system.

If we wish to perceive the subtle energies carried by sound, words and music for any extended period of time, we must protect our ears at all times in order to penetrate into the sphere of profound listening. We use sunglasses to protect our eyes from harsh light. Unfortunately, no such thing exists to protect the ears. It is up to us to develop enough awareness to avoid damaging noise. Frequent exposure to noise levels beyond 90 decibels (dB) causes irreversible cellular lesions that, on the anatomic level, result in micro-hemorrhaging in the cochlea and, on the symptomatic level, a definitive loss of hearing.

The decibel is the scientific unit of measurement for sound: *deci,* for one-tenth, and *bel,* for Alexander Graham Bell, the inventor of the telephone. A sound ten times louder than another is said to be 10 dB higher, and for each tenfold increase in intensity the sound level increases by 10 dB. Thus, a sound one thousand times more intense than another is 30 dB stronger; a sound one hundred thousand times more intense is 50 dB stronger.

Scientist Claude Illouz describes the effect of high decibel levels on the ears:

> From 120 dB and beyond (a normal rock concert) the sound blast has the same effect as a deflagration. It is not rare for the eardrum membrane to tear like the skin of a drum being pounded too violently. Total deafness immediately ensues, accompanied by acoustical phenomena, such as a continuous whistling and ringing in the ears which persists for several weeks before decreasing and then disappearing, sometimes only partially. The inner ear conceals 28,000 vibratory filaments—and not one more. These highly refined cells are miniature, extremely sophisticated computers. Each has its own particular function, selecting information, analyzing sounds, breaking down frequencies before sending through the auditory nerve, an extremely reliable electro-acoustical program, easily decoded by the brain.... The more powerful and sharp the sound, the more it is likely to damage the filaments which, unfortunately, do not have the power to regenerate themselves. Obviously, the fewer filaments there are, the less efficient the ear. [11]

We should be careful to protect the auditory nerve if we wish to enjoy concentration, equilibrium, vigilance and attention. Moreover, lesions in the inner ear are permanent and irreversible. Blood no longer flows to the parts of the cochlea where necrosis is present; this is cellular death. Hearing aids are designed for the middle ear only (to lessen the effect of lesions on the eardrum and/or the small bones in the middle ear) and because they amplify sounds, they only increase damage levels. We should be forewarned.

> If we wish to perceive the subtle energies carried by sound, words and music for any extended period of time, we must protect our ears at all times in order to penetrate into the sphere of profound listening.

When noise becomes too loud, we should immediately take action to protect our fragile ears. The ear is the organ of equilibrium. Beyond 90 decibels vertigo, memory trouble and sometimes depression can occur.

Noise can be defined as a sound that is loud, unpleasant or undesired. In the U.S., federal regulations are in place to limit the level of noise in the workplace and protect employees from lowered productivity and injury. For some, producing noise is a sign of power. This is why noise has become the scourge of the twentieth century. According to some estimates, for an industrialized country with a population of approximately 50 million, annual health care costs directly attributable to the effects of noise reach the $5 billion level—the same amount of money it takes to fight the harmful effects of smoke addiction.

These figures are probably underestimated, as many sick people cannot properly determine the cause of their illnesses. Furthermore, many doctors are not yet fully aware of the physical and psychological wounds caused by the shrill of ultra sensitive antitheft alarms, the thunderous jolts of motorcycles equipped with illegal mufflers, the invading rattle of pneumatic drills, the howls of police, firefighting and ambulance sirens, and the virtually unbearable levels of overamplified music. What's more, now we have the ubiquitous sounds of a plethora of different cell phone rings to contend with.

Directly or indirectly, noise contributes to the progression of mental illnesses. By rocking our composition until it reaches a state of imbalance, noise subtly attacks our nervous system, unleashing fatigue, dizziness, ulcers, cardiovascular problems, unhealthy behavioral patterns, hormonal imbalances and depression, if it does not actually lead to sheer madness. A sizeable portion of the 45 million Americans who regularly suffer from headaches point to noise as one of the factors that trigger pain. According to the *American Medical News*, roughly $10 million a day is lost to related productivity decreases in the workplace.[12] Further, according to the National Institute of Public Health in the Czech Republic, the consumption of sedative and hypnotic prescription medicines is significantly higher in noisy areas.[13] There is no physiological tolerance to noise; in other words, the living being endures its effects without ever becoming accustomed to it.

Given the warnings posed by these statistics, we can rightfully wonder if one of the most widely broadcast types of music in industrialized countries is not also the greatest source of cellular disorders. New illnesses, often attributed to "civilization," are generally caused by pollution. Along with chemical and psychological pollution, we now have sound pollution.

If we were to take a measuring device to a rock

concert or rave where sound systems are boosted to the limit, the device would easily register peak levels of 120 to 140 decibels! This is beyond the pain threshold and could potentially result in lesions. Other forms of music listening can be problematic. People often listen to headphones at high volumes over prolonged periods of time. According to a 1996 study cited by the Canadian Association of Speech-Language Pathologists and Audiologists, this also causes damage. When subjects are so totally immersed in sound, loss of vigilance, loss of balance and nausea have been detected.[14] Furthermore, it would seem that the ability to perceive physical parameters, for example, accurately estimating distance or depth, might be altered.

In 1985, Annie Moch, a lecturer at the University of Paris Psychology Department, published an extensively researched study on the subject of hearing loss. Research she conducted in the United States indicates that the temporary hearing loss that occurs after a subject is exposed to high noise levels should not normally go beyond 10 decibels over a period of two minutes after the exposure; otherwise, permanent deafness will ensue, especially if

the trauma is repeated successively. However, Dr. Moch's measurements carried out before and after the audition of rock concerts—or recorded music—show a loss of hearing that reaches the 30-decibel level among teenagers aged 16 to 18 years.[15]

In a study on noise warfare and music that deafens, researcher Richard Cannavo noted that examining the hearing of musicians could provide a good indication of the effects of high noise levels. He states: "Out of 43 rock professionals examined by scientists, an average loss of hearing of 20 dB was noted after six years of activity."[16] Even classical musicians must be careful. Specialists who examined the 110 musicians of the Swiss Orchestra assert that nearly half of them exhibited hearing impairment and 30 percent suffered from ringing in the ears and even vertigo.[17]

Millions of teenagers suffer from hearing impairment caused by exposure to music at excessive volumes. This is what makes Richard Cannavo comment: "How very ironic! At a time when music reigns supreme, when it is omnipresent and universal, we see the advent of a generation of deaf children."[18]

Dr. Illouz explains that the level of intensity and the length of the listening period are closely linked to degenerative mechanisms. Sound vibrations of very short duration, if they are extremely intense, are enough to cause acoustic trauma. Conversely, a prolonged noise can result in permanent lesions even if it is of relatively low intensity. It is important to note that amplifying systems currently in use often produce noise levels of well beyond 120 decibels, particularly in the case of bass notes. Considering the fact that concerts sometimes last a full two hours, it is easy to understand why so many people currently suffer from major hearing trouble.

The problem is compounded by the fact that we remain ignorant of our growing deafness. We can safely say that the residents of huge modern cities suffer from hearing impairment and all the imbalances it causes at the cellular level. Prescription medications are not the solution for coping with the anxiety and stress of modern life. Rather, the solution should be a regimen of silence, of strolls in nature with birdsong and babbling brooks. The medical prescription should also include music with the power to relax (as demonstrated in serious studies), inspired meditative melodies and all sound vibrations able to heal the troubles linked to exposure to noise.

In order to perceive the song of atoms or the subtle electromagnetic energy of the life spectrum, today's human beings should stop making unnecessary noise. Without this voluntary gesture, people will remain deaf to vibrations of their timeless souls. As Marie-Louise Aucher writes in the chapter entitled "Psychophysiology and Psychophony" in her book *Sonorous Man:*

> Whoever has seen a little white mouse, submitted even for only a few seconds to a very loud siren, suffer an audiogenic epileptic seizure, lethal in sensitive subjects, will have understood that noise is more than an annoying sensation which we grow accustomed to, more than a source of professional deafness, but the major factor

behind nervous imbalance in the modern world. The convulsive effect is accompanied by a general disturbance at the visceral level and by neurotic disorders. The psychophysiologist explains this by localizing the action of the noises in the unifying and regulating centers of the brain stem, centers of the body's wisdom (including the brain of the spirit), which become the centers of the body's madness.[19]

Despite the now widespread practice of prescribing medications to counteract the madness of the world today, perhaps in the near future new doctors will be more interested in their patients' well-being than in the growth of the pharmaceutical industry. The music of the soul, unlike medication, does not run counter to the Hippocratic oath.

COWS THAT LOVE MOZART

In scientific circles, the norm is to collect data from experiments on plants before using animals as subjects. When effects on fauna, flora and animals are evident, experiments are conducted on human subjects. Let us examine this scientific integrity, keeping in mind the following findings, as described by Rolando Benenzon:

An Illinois farmer planted the exact same type of seeds in two greenhouses, under identical fertility, humidity and temperature conditions. In one greenhouse, he placed a speaker, which broadcast music 24 hours a day. After a while, he noticed that in the building where music was played, the corn crop had sprouted more rapidly, kernels weighed more and the earth was more fertile; plants closest to the speaker were damaged from the effect of sound vibration. The experiment proved to be so successful that in Canada music is currently used in several agricultural operations. It has been observed that sound vibrations destroy a microorganism (parasite), which is harmful to corn crops. In veterinary medicine, it is often laughingly said that cows love Mozart but on the other hand, that Wagner or jazz decreases their milk production. In American research centers, however, the issue is under serious study. Illinois statistics show that the milk production of cows kept in stables close to airports where jets take off and land decreases to zero because of the surrounding noise level.[20]

If you dip a tuning fork vibrating at exactly 440 cycles per second into a glass of water, you are sure to get wet, because on contact with the water, the tuning fork will produce a cascade of splashes. In laboratories, the tuning fork has long since been replaced by electronic sound generators, which have become the instruments of psychophysics. If the vibrations of a simple tuning fork can produce a cascade of splashes, what is the power held by the vibrations emanating from a symphony orchestra or a rock music recording?

Clearly, all musical sources produce a measurable and quantifiable power that influences us. Music affects plants, animals and human beings. It conditions them to behave in certain ways. It "programs" them in one sense or another. The use of melodic and rhythmic sound vibration is an age-old practice, turned to since time immemorial to maintain or transform the level of consciousness, and subsequently to reestablish equilibrium in the body as well as the mind.

We can no longer ignore the powerful effects of every type of sound on life in general. Whether we like it or not, whether we are conscious of it or not, this vibrating force pervades us. It jams itself into our systems, settles in each of our cells and spreads its destructive or creative power, harmful or beneficial influence. Some forms of music have the power to make us more aggressive, while others can bring out our gentler instincts. Just as electricity can produce both cold and heat, music can be the driving force behind peace or war.

The force of music is a neutral energy; we are responsible for its ultimate effect. We should shoulder the responsibility of our own desires; we should be aware of what we really want. If it's violence we want, then let us listen to aggressive-sounding music. But if it's peace, then let us surround ourselves with soft and calming music. The choice is ours: to assault our body, mind and spirit with heavy, violent vibrations or nourish them with pure waves and high frequencies. Hélène Caya, at the end of her groundbreaking book *From Sound Springs Light* states: "The gentler music is, the more love it transmits."[21]

> We can no longer ignore the powerful effects of every type of sound on life in general. Whether we like it or not, whether we are conscious of it or not, this vibrating force pervades us.

Being gentle in no way precludes being strong. True strength is not a momentary state of excitement that consumes our reserves. On the contrary, it is a gentle and irresistible energy, luminous and powerful. On this level, nothing is good and nothing is bad. It is up to each of us to recognize what we want to achieve by listening to a particular musical energy, to develop the sensitivity required to feel its effects on our bodies and our minds.

All we need do is listen attentively, refuse to submit blindly to the influence of vibrations, and examine our

reactions when music's invisible waves reach us. Are we
nervous? Are we calm? Do we want to remain in a state
of nervous tension? After this analysis, a decision is imperative. If we judge that a certain type of musical wave
produces harmful effects on us, causing nervous fatigue,
aggression or lack of concentration, nothing prevents us
from suppressing the source whenever it is possible to
do so. Nothing prevents us from turning off the radio or
the television or changing stations or channels. Nothing
prevents us from leaving a place where music we deem
inadequate is being played. It is a matter of free will.

MUSIC INFLUENCES OUR FEELINGS

Joseph Stuessy, a music professor at the University of Texas in San Antonio, tells us to be on guard: "All music, whatever it may be, influences our mood, our feelings, our attitudes and the behavior it causes."[22]

The *Song of Songs,* a Biblical account that is one of the most beautiful love songs ever written, tells the story of the love of a Sulamite woman for a young shepherd. King Solomon, who in vain exerts all his wisdom and glory to try to conquer the young woman's heart, threatened their union. Wishing to remain faithful to her shepherd, the Sulamite woman urges her female companions not to awaken in her the lure for the king who seeks to win her heart. Recognizing that certain words had the power to transform her desires and that the behavior that would result from listening to these words would inevitably conflict with her true feelings, she refuses to listen.

What should we make of this attitude and the valuable teaching it holds in light of the songs with which our ears are saturated day and night? Whatever the musical genre, many "commercial" songs are successful with a large listening audience who are ignorant of the music's long-term effects on its listeners. These songs are broadcast numerous times a day, thereby creating impression upon impression in the listener's mind. Such a bombardment of sound affects the function of the brain, and its reactions are directly linked to the emotional intention that the songwriters, composers and performers have chosen, consciously or not, to inject into their creation.

We should not hastily conclude that all popular songs are harmful. It cannot be denied that artists sometimes compose works that inspire us spiritually and rhythms that elevate and stimulate the body's energies. The cumulative effect of these highly inspired melodies is therefore beneficial. Songs that carry authentic feelings, and amount to more than mindless mechanical repetition with a few superimposed chords, tend to restore the peace and harmony of the soul.

There is just cause for concern, however, when we consider the violent nature of the words of certain "hits." These lyrics, whether truly sung or bellowed, are nevertheless honest in their intentions. They do not suggest but directly propose to their willing listeners the clamor of anxiety and cries of agony. What devastation these sounds create in the mind!

> Songs that carry authentic feelings, and amount to more than mindless mechanical repetition with a few superimposed chords, tend to restore the peace and harmony of the soul.

Fortunately, living beings always have the privilege of reform, of redirecting themselves toward influences linked to the divine plan, or at least to the virtuous forces of nature. While the effect is theoretically reversible, the harm has temporarily been done. Although what is supposedly harmful can eventually become beneficial in the evolutionary sense—because every obstacle can be seen as a stepping stone—the fact remains that the sociological reactions caused by harmful influences strongly tend toward violence, base sensuality and depressive nihilism. When the musical theme and the lyrics produce joy, hope, healthy confidence and love without expectations, then there is no contraindication, as the mind is favorably influenced and the individual and society benefit.

Many scientific works have been written on psycho-acoustics (the psychological effects of sound) and they can be used as a source of reference for investigating this subject. Unfortunately, many of these works are written in a specialist's jargon. It is not necessary, however, to be an expert in the matter to sense the different effects of sound vibrations on the mind and body. It is enough to close our eyes, let the determined energy of the music permeate our beings and allow its effect to overwhelm us. Even if the secrets of the theories of therapeutic music, of neurology or of musical semantics are unknown to us, our inner voice (some people refer to it as our common sense) will respond to music with one of three major reactions, depending on three types of feelings we can perceive.

Reference to these three groups of feelings can be found in the Sanskrit text the Bhagavad Gita.[23] This timeless text clearly shows how humans are condi-tioned by certain forces, or modes (gunas), inherent in the physical plane. These forces fall into three main cat-egories: the force of ignorance (tama), the force of pas-sion (raja) and the force of virtue (sattva). According to the Gita, all material nature is composed of these three energies.[24] When living beings encounter physical na-ture, they are systematically conditioned by it. Thus, a combination of these three modes influences everyone born into this world. At times, a mixture of passion and ignorance will compel them to react in a certain man-ner. At other times, virtue and passion will influence them to react differently.

All material things, including culture and art, are directed by these energies, and music is no exception. A composition is always permeated by nature's three modes and, consequently, it influences the listener through the corresponding energy in that person. This is known as the phenomenon of resonance. It is possible to discern the energies present in musical vibrations. Whether we are willing or not, whether we are aware or not, these energies act incessantly upon our patterns of behavior, our tastes, our attitudes, our personalities and, ultimately, our destinies. The sensations we can experience while under the influence of a given musical energy are many, but they can be classified according to three principal groups that correspond to the three gunas:

1. The Musical Energies of Ignorance

Such music makes us feel indolent, insensitive, indifferent and inert. We feel exhausted and completely unenergetic. We become lazy, inactive and lethargic. We sink into a stupor, an uncaring attitude...a depression. We lack the will to take action; we lack enthusiasm. We feel pessimistic and negative, that nothing is of any importance. We feel that we are harboring illusions. Everything is dark and obscure. These musical energies draw out the ignorance, or inertia, within us.

2. The Musical Energies of Passion

This type of music arouses in us the thirst of limitless burning desires. We feel growing in our hearts the signs of deep attachment, selfish ambitions and uncontrollable desires. It makes us feel greedy. These musical energies inspire within us emotions linked to the mode of passion.

3. The Musical Energies of Virtue

This type of music calms us, relaxes us, but does not make us drowsy. It soothes while stimulating us. It makes us more self-confident and helps us concentrate. It elevates our thoughts to beauty, goodness, truth and honesty. It elevates us toward superior realities, toward love, toward God. It enlightens us and brings us a sense of happiness. We feel a stream of purifying light enter us through all the doors of the body. These musical energies fill us with virtue.

At times, the mode of passion dominates and drives away virtue and its influence. At other times, virtue predominates over passion. And at still other times, the guna of ignorance triumphs over virtue and passion. In this manner, the three energies constantly compete with one another. The Vedic scriptures show how extensively the three modes of material nature are involved in all of the world's activities. To escape from the spell of the three gunas is to free oneself from the limits imposed by the material atmosphere. Thus, incarnated individuals who are able to transcend these forces liberate themselves from the yoke of death and rebirth and from relentless anxieties associated with this karmic cycle and are thus able to enjoy exquisite happiness in this life. Those who are aware of this reality strive to listen to music that either cultivates virtue or goes beyond all three modes of energy, transcending virtue, passion and ignorance.

The latter part of this text discusses how sound energies contained in the vibrations of specific mantras, when chanted or heard, can lead us toward a virtuous art of living marked by peace, health, equilibrium and happiness. Additionally, it covers how the sounds of the Holy Names contain an energy form (in Sanskrit, *param shakti,* superior inner energy) that has the power to thwart the ill effects of the three modes of material nature. Music with the transcendental power to go beyond virtue, passion and ignorance can gradually deliver its listeners from the chains that bind them within the narrow confines of their physical selves. Such music unlocks the door to our inner selves and propels us toward the immeasurable vastness of the life of the soul.

HEARING AND NUTRITION

Given the power of music to help us achieve a state of balance in our lives and to develop body, mind and spirit, it is important that we do what we can to both protect and to improve our hearing. It is, in fact, possible to modify or improve our hearing by altering our nutritional habits.

Aveline and Michio Kushi, authors of the book *Macrobiotic Pregnancy and Care of the Newborn,* mention in their studies that when a newborn's ears are small, pointed at the top and located high on the head, this is a sign of the mother's excessive consumption of animal products during pregnancy.[25] When insufficiently developed, the auricle—the visible part of the ear—is unable to concentrate and orient sound toward the entrance of the auditory meatus in an adequate manner, appreciably diminishing the intensity of waves on the extremely taut membrane of the eardrum. The importance of the external ear's development is demonstrated in nature by a little desert fox, the fennec, which roams about the Sahara at night. Its large pointed ears catch the faintest sounds made by its prey in the dark.

> The music of the soul cannot be heard by an ear overloaded with fermentations resulting from the digestion of animal flesh.

We see on the one hand (with the example of the fennec) that the external ear's development constitutes an important factor in the quality of hearing, and on the other hand (through the research of the Kushis) that proper or improper ear development is determined before birth, by the mother's nutritional habits. To support proper ear development in the fetus, the Kushis advise pregnant women to refrain, at least during pregnancy, from eating animal food products (meat, fish and eggs), with the exception of dairy products. They also state that the fear of protein deficiency due to meat deprivation is unfounded, and that if people wish to enjoy both good hearing and good physical and psychological health during their lifetime, it is strongly recommended that they refrain from eating animal flesh.

In their research on cancer and nutrition, Chantal Drolet and Anne-Marie Sicotte remind us that the 20th century brought radical nutritional changes to the general population in industrialized countries. An over consumption of fat, particularly from animals, is undoubtedly the most dangerous of these innovations. In "Nutritional Habits that Kill," published in *Resource Guide* magazine, Drolet and Sicotte state, "International studies prove that meat and animal fat are the foods most likely to create a favorable environment for cancer."[26] So indeed, there appears to be a link between cancer, music, good hearing and our nutritional habits!

Music can have an effect, can soothe and even heal in some instances. It remains impotent and ineffective, however, if we as listeners do not take fate into our own hands. If we continue gorging ourselves in an anarchic way, with no respect for the laws of nature, we will only partially perceive the subtle energies of the rhythm and harmony that can cure us. How can we enjoy good hearing (what to speak of the gift of *clairaudience*, or the ability to hear subtle energies) when the colon's function is impaired and the liver and the body's cells cannot sustain the required level of detoxification to keep the body running well?

As early as 1893, German physician Louis Kuhne, in his book *The New Science of Healing,* demonstrated the common elements of illnesses and the logic of a vegetarian regimen. He reasoned that the cause of illness is the body's congestion with pathogenic products resulting from poor digestion of animal-derived foods. Poor nutrition leads to poor digestion, and poor digestion, in turn, results in the dispersal of foreign substances, fermented and gaseous, throughout the body. These foreign substances, generated for the most part by the consumption of animal flesh, are gradually deposited in areas of the body, beginning in the vicinity of the secretory organs. As time goes on and poor digestion persists, congestion increases and extends to more remote locations, mainly the upper part of the body, notably the neck, the head, and of course, the ears.

When the ears are affected, it means the entire body is suffering from an overload of fermented substances. When these congesting substances make their way to the ears (connected to the trachea by the Eustachian tubes), the delicate organ of hearing is obstructed and hardens, fine lesions appear on the eardrum and it can no longer vibrate normally under the action of sound waves. This results in a catarrh of the ear, an inflammation of the mucous membrane and hypersecretion of the glands.

As Dr. Kuhne explains:

> Pathogenic products from the consumption of animal flesh are deposited particularly in the center of the ear. It often happens that acute cases occur and the pressure from below is very strong. Actual purulent abscesses form in the interior of the ear, which must constantly eliminate pus and foreign substances in fermentation, producing the substances that everyone is familiar with. If this acute case is not cured in time and naturally, the consequence is an ever-increasing accumulation of morbid substances and often even the direct destruction of the hearing organ whose condition deteriorates when one attempts to address its acute state with medication.[27]

To better understand what happens in the ear when the body is overloaded, it's necessary to understand the importance of the Eustachian tubes, named after the Italian anatomist Bartolomeo Eustachio. The tubes equalize the air pressure on both sides of the eardrum, which is sensitive to sound vibrations. This compensation process is automatic and goes undetected, as pressure changes are usually progressive. Abrupt pressure changes, as during an aircraft landing or when coming down several floors in an elevator, can be felt until one swallows or yawns to open the Eustachian tubes, allowing the air pressure to reach proper levels.

The Eustachian tubes are incapable of equalizing pressure when an overload of morbid substances obstructs them, as occurs during the common cold, an infection or chronic poor digestion. The pressure in the middle ear reaches a level below that of exterior pressure because surrounding tissue gradually absorbs the air in the middle ear. Uneven pressure on the eardrum dampens hearing; sounds seem to be filtered through cotton wool. With a vegetarian diet, it is possible to avoid the ear problems resulting from poor digestion of animal products and the subsequent body-wide overload of morbid substances.

In addition, eating a diet of fruit, vegetables, and whole cereals elevates the body and mind and enables us to listen to the great universal vibrations constantly coming toward us, but which we cannot hear when our ears are obstructed. The music of the soul cannot be heard by an ear overloaded with fermentations resulting from the digestion of animal flesh. Carnivorous humanity becomes powerless to perceive the higher truths of the self and is prevented from gaining access to the influence of miraculous celestial vibrations. "Gastronomic" dishes, laden with pain, make the human being deaf to the subtle call of the soul's musical energies.

By following a nutritional regimen that is in harmony with the laws of the universe and respectful of life, we open ourselves to the highest sensory perceptions and to higher experiences. We penetrate the infinite world of virtue. Our eyes no longer see the same colors. Our ears detect nature's most subtle sounds. The wind in the clouds, the breeze murmuring among the leaves, and the rhythm of the fountain become the most wonderful of symphonies. The doors of contemplation and meditation are wide open to us and we discover the astonishing music of the inner self.

A meatless diet facilitates the opening of the "third ear," the organ of clairaudience. This subtle organ vibrates at a much higher speed than the physical ear, and, once developed, provides access to the universe of profound listening, of listening to the self, where we perceive the finest form of music: the music of the soul.

Inner music generates a genuine feeling of plenitude and is the basis of physical and spiritual healing. As long as humans go on ruthlessly killing living creatures they consider inferior, they will know neither health nor peace and will be unable to perceive the subtle vibrations of the music of the soul. French physician Paul Carton is adamant on this point: "As long as men slaughter animals, they will continue to kill one another. He who sows the seeds of murder and pain cannot expect to harvest love and joy. The habits

of killing and of eating meat are incompatible with the hope of universal happiness and complete wisdom."[28]

> Today's musicians and composers have a responsibility beyond simply playing or writing music. They have the responsibility of being aware of how their creativity affects the individuals who are subject to its consequences, whether good or bad.

To be aware of the celestial music of the spheres, as Pythagoras called this genuine panacea for the present afflictions suffered by humanity, it is useful to submit to certain nutritional rules and choose foods that make the soul as pure as possible. Vegetarianism helps us gain access to purification on the spiritual, animistic and physical levels—a purification that was probably practiced by Hermes' students in antiquity.

In certain parts of the world, survival obviously depends on the ability to hunt; when truly necessary, eating meat should not be rejected outright. But at the present time, animals are slaughtered industrially, in an atmosphere of unthinkable terror. As a result, their carcasses are electrified with fear, horror, aggression, anger and revolt. Our contemporaries do not merely absorb meat, but unknowingly they feed on all these harmful feelings, along with all that this may imply for the health of their subtle and physical bodies.

Many scientists and thinkers have realized the imminent danger for the evolution of humanity that industrial consumption of animal flesh constitutes. Albert Einstein, a physicist of unequaled genius, ardently defended vegetarianism. In his writings on personal development, he stated, "Vegetarianism, by its purely physical action on human nature, could be a very beneficial influence on humanity's destiny."[29]

America's beloved philosopher, Henry David Thoreau, was of the same opinion: "I am convinced that the destiny of the human race, in its gradual evolution, calls for a stop to the consumption of animal flesh, just as in the same way, wild tribesmen stopped devouring one another once they came into contact with more civilized beings."[30] The horrible discordance of slaughterhouses gives rise to an uninterrupted series of false notes in the great evolutionary music of humankind. To conclude this examination of the relationship between hearing, evolution and nutrition, consider the opinion of Dr. Paul Carton, who has extensively studied Pythagoras' theories on music and life in general:

"The Pythagorean diet is a powerful factor in higher human evolution because it ensures the most perfect and harmonious performance of the spiritual, vital and physical life forces. First of all, it purifies the mind by sparing it from incitements toward brutality and sensuality. It fosters better intellectual development because it undoubtedly facilitates proper brain functioning. All individuals who

abandon the use of meat are amazed to see how their minds become more lucid, their clairvoyant abilities greater and their objectives loftier. Gentleness, optimism, composure and the sheer joy of living increase progressively. The individual feels transported into a superior world because he has liberated his brain from unhealthy influences, strengthened his moral sense, widened the horizons of his thoughts, facilitated the education of his willpower and increased his spiritual value."[31]

Not only does what we eat affect our digestion and in turn our listening, but what we listen to while we eat can also influence our digestion. In his book *The Doctor Prescribes Music,* physicist Edward Podolsky considers the value of listening to music during meals. In his opinion, beautiful music played during a meal is of great help in facilitating the digestive process. In his work he describes a scientific discovery that claims that the principal nerve of the eardrum (middle ear) ends at the center of the tongue; it is linked to the brain, and reacts to both taste and sound impulses.[32]

Commenting on this scientific report, Hal A. Lingerman, in *The Healing Energies of Music,* states that it is no longer possible to ignore the close relationship that exists between healthy food and appropriate music.[33] It is not by pure chance that in ancient cultures, expert musicians were invited to play soft and pleasant melodies during meals and feasts.

Recall that when unpleasant emotions are felt, the pylorus, a muscular structure situated at the base of the stomach, closes. The stomach's contents can no longer reach the bowel. There follows a bloated sensation, a heaviness that occurs while digestive acids stop working. The result is drowsiness and irritability.

Professor Podolsky notes, "Music is the best antidote for unpleasantness at the dinner table. When there is music to be heard, there is an outpouring of gastric juices. They act as a flushing device. Food is properly digested and it passes from the stomach into the duodenum through a wide-open pylorus."[34]

During meals, music should be simple and joyful, with neither great contrasts nor intellectual or emotional complexities. Hal Lingerman particularly recommends the flute and the harp as sources of this type of music.

Personally, I have observed that the music said to be of the Versailles School, which includes the works of Lully, Couperin and Delalande (*Symphonies for the King's Dinners*), creates a climate of peace, joy and majesty that is altogether appropriate to accompany the sacred act of nourishment.

> Not only does what we eat affect our digestion and in turn our listening, but what we listen to while we eat can also influence our digestion.

The Vedic scriptures proclaim, "Spiritual awakening begins with the tongue." By transforming the otherwise banal act of eating into a conscious offering to the Divine, the more sordid impulses of the senses can be sublimated. Through the nature of our nutrition and the attitude with which we feed ourselves, we can either open or close the crystalline doors of the music of the soul.

THE PURIFYING POWER OF LOVE

As we have seen, virtuous nutrition can facilitate refined hearing and listening. The Bhagavad Gita stipulates that a spiritual nutrition has the power to purify the sensory organs, to produce finer cerebral tissues and to clarify thoughts.[35] Spiritual nutrition goes beyond simple vegetarianism and lays claim to the purifying power of love: "If, with love and devotion, I am offered a leaf, a flower, a fruit or some water, I will accept it."[36]

Here, the ultimate devotional aspect of the God-force, Krishna, the mystical poet of the Bhagavad Gita, reveals that the sanctification of food opens the doors to inner sound. The main factor, the principal ingredient in the preparation of such a selfless gesture, is the thirst for absolute love. Indeed, the infinite energy that penetrates all things has no need for food!

The body is a temple. If we respect it, it will vibrate in harmony with the Absolute. It will sing in unison with the beauty of the Infinite.

a new musical aesthetic

> The composer, in particular, sets out on a journey
> on uncharted waters while he awaits inspiration.
> What he receives can elevate and inspire just as it
> can have the opposite type of influence. His respon-
> sibility is great, although he is often unaware that
> he bears it.[37]
>
> —From Cyril Scott's *Music: Its Secret*
> *Influence through the Ages*

Based on either research, the latest accomplishments of music therapy experts, or intuition, many people now perceive the urgent need to reorient music composition. Whether they are spiritual aspirants, specialists, musicians, music lovers or simply listeners, they have concluded that establishing a new musical aesthetic is essential. Psychoacoustics, which was practiced by many ancient civilizations, is resurfacing for application in the modern world.

More research is under way with a view to better understand the human reaction to the phenomenon of sound. The time for such work has indeed come. In a world where omnipresent sound pollution is a source of disequilibrium and illness, it is imperative that sound itself be used as a balancing and regenerative element. Therefore, today's musicians and composers have a responsibility beyond simply playing or writing music. They have the responsibility of being aware of how their creativity affects individuals, those who are subject to its consequences, whether good or bad. Musicians and composers are responsible for their music, as gardeners are responsible for the fruit grown on the trees under their care. If a tree's fruit is poisoned, what does the gardener do? If the tree is beyond saving, the wise gardener cuts it down to prevent the disease from spreading to the other trees.

The great wisdom of the universe acts in the same way toward societies and empires. When their fruit is no longer healthy, they are eliminated. And what is art in general—and music in particular—if not the most evident fruit of any human civilization, the fruit that best reflects each civilization's desires, inclinations and states of being? Viewed from the perspective that the objective of existence is to elevate the individual through science, philosophy and art, it becomes obvious that humanity must empower itself to choose a musical form that favors spiritual life and global reharmonization.

Great music is always simple. If it is too sophisticated, it fails to move us. All that occurs in this case is a type of sterile and disheartening intellectual excitation. In *Invitation to Music*, Roland de Candé has this to say on the subject: "The great music of the modern era is much more difficult to play than the music of other eras. The average amateur pianist is unable to play anything composed by Boulez or Stockhausen, nor even the works of Schoenberg or Webern. Part of today's music is even so difficult to play that it demands specialized performers. It is not for me to say whether this is good or bad. It is quite an extraordinary fact. Today's music, with its difficulties, cannot hope to be classical tomorrow."[38]

To experience the transformative effects of musical energies, we need to search for a harmonious art of living and a type of music that does not call for intellectual analysis but, rather, directly touches the deepest recesses of the heart—music that speaks directly to the soul.

It is urgent that we come to understand to what extent ritualistic, sacred, meditative or devotional music can heal us and provide an effective solution to the disruptive and unbalancing effects suffered by human civilization. In addition, we should attempt to comprehend the extent to which it helps us rediscover the voice of the heart by guiding us toward higher spheres of life, those from which we originate, regardless of our race or religious beliefs. Then, its true role is unveiled and we discover the music of the soul. It provides links that bind one human being to another by providing them with the means to discover their true spiritual identity. Finally, it provides the means of establishing a relationship between the inner self and the complete whole that is Divinity, of which the music of the soul is an integral part and whose qualities it shares.

Be this as it may, it is not easy to be selective about what we listen to today. Music is ubiquitous: in the street, in shops, in banks, on public transit, at the office, at home, everywhere. We could say that we play an unwilling part in our lack of sound constraint. Though music is one of the most powerful vehicles of social change, it is used anywhere, by anyone, in the most offhand manner. As previously discussed, the power of the decibel has been savagely unleashed upon us.

Some physicians have sounded the alarm and, fortunately, we are witnessing a counterattack on noise: more and more music lovers are turning to more acoustic, softer, more ethereal music—to music that is pleasing to the soul.

Healer and spiritual guide Mikhaël Aïvanhov states:

"Ordinary music awakens human passions. Thus, as soon as it begins to play, we feel pushed to idiocies, we become a little mad. A few young people have admitted as much to me. Upon hearing it, they are ready to embark on any adventure. This music excites them; it drives them quite mad. When will we turn to music that provides a link with the spiritual world, music that calms, appeases and inspires?"[39]

Music that calms, appeases and inspires can soothe the world. No words can be compared to this music. Our religious traditions tell us to be honest, to be kind and to treat others as we would like to be treated ourselves. But these words do not necessarily penetrate the heart. Often, they remain on the surface and the concepts they represent are not integrated into our lives. On the other hand, music that calms and appeases produces an impression in the thought process, and this impression, in turn, enters the heart. We come to desire the realization within us and around us, the image of health, beauty, peace, kindness and purity that we have perceived. We make the decision to live what had hitherto remained only on the surface of our being.

Instrumental music, like meditative song, represents a vibration that offers the advantage of not being expressed with comprehensible words likely to arouse impulses inconsistent with our true nature. In the state of mental peace, the spirit of opposition has no opportunity to assert itself. In this way, listening to sounds that are suggestive of physical or moral qualities can facilitate the acquisition of those very qualities.

THE ANTIDOTE DECIBEL: THE SONG OF NATURE

As with healing music, the antidote against the apocalyptic noises in our environment can be found in nature. Nature's song is the easiest road to the abstract garden of harmony. When we become more sensitive to the natural beauty that surrounds us, we feel closer to the divine intelligence that holds sway over the elements. What results is a harmonization of all the body's cells. This state produces an incomparable sensation that is capable of healing all modifications or injuries that noise has upon us.

A waterfall can make more noise than a combustion engine; but while the latter exhausts, the former soothes. The rumble of ocean tides is not less deafening than the 90 or 100 decibels of rush-hour traffic, yet it relaxes. Identical decibel levels are found elsewhere as well. Played equally loudly, a heavy metal rock song seems much more intense than a Mozart concerto, but both produce and emit the same number of decibels.

LIFE IS LISTENING

The same compositions, or harmonic and rhythmic arrangements of identical nature, always generate the same emotions and feelings. Here lies the greatest threat and the greatest opportunity. Certain feelings are awakened by music and the experience can be relived several times over. These emotions create habits and the habits in turn shape the personality. Our characters create our destinies.

The basic nature of the music we listen to invariably leaves its imprint on our customs, actions and patterns of behavior. Music imitates life, and life imitates music. It is therefore important to be aware of the sound we are exposing ourselves too. In reality, the volume of sound should be regulated at all times.

Monitoring the sound to which we are exposed needs to be extended to babies in the womb, as well. This need is supported by both ancient texts and modern research. We find in the authentic commentary on the *Vedanta Sutra,* the *Srimad Bhagavatam* (or *Bhagavat Purana),* written by Vyasadev some 5,000 years ago, several accounts that demonstrate how the fetus is capable of hearing sounds from without. Vyasdev, the compiler of the Vedas, instructed his very own son, Sukadev Goswami, in the science of *bhakti yoga*

while he was still in his mother's womb.

According to the *Brahma-vaivarta Purana,* Sukadev Goswami was a liberated soul freed from earthly concerns even before birth. His father, Vyasadev, sensing that his son would not remain in his company after birth, saw to

it that the child, although still in his mother's womb, would hear the message that he had to transmit to instruct him on the principles of inner life.

In the *Bhagavatam,* a vast historical fresco, the story of Prahlad also shows to what extent the fetus is able to perceive words spoken in the pregnant mother's presence. Hiranyakashipu, a man of demonic temperament, had sired the child Prahlad. While his mother was residing at the monastery of the sage-musician Narada Muni, the latter spoke at length of devotional philosophy. According to the text, Prahlad had not only heard the great musician's comments, but he had grasped them. A few years later, he was able to repeat the message he had heard before birth to his classmates, greatly angering his father.

These two references that date back several thousands of years suggest that humankind has always been aware of the effects of song and words on the living being, particularly on the fetus. It is worthy of note that Sanskrit verses are poetic texts of great beauty, with elaborate rhythms and metrics. For the most part, they are still sung. When we have the opportunity to read or hear these verses, we can understand somewhat the vibrations of joy and peace that these children could feel, even prior to leaving the womb.

In scientific circles, it has become more and more evident that sound waves affect the fetus. Researchers have been astonished to discover the extent to which exterior noises reach the unborn child. Intra-uterine microphones clearly pick up a whole range of noises. Further, a recent study published in *Psychological Science* holds that the fetus learns to recognize its mother's voice while in utero, and can distinguish her voice from others upon birth.[40]

Among other researchers, Conrad Lorenz established that shortly before birth, sounds are heard and interpreted by living beings. His experiences with birds led him to talk to ducks' eggs on a regular basis. After they hatched, he noticed that the ducklings would come toward him whenever he spoke, as if they already knew him well. Other scientists working with chicks, and even with human fetuses, who grew accustomed to their father's voice during the gestation period, confirmed the results of this particular experiment.

> In speaking to their as yet unborn child, the mother and father should speak to the eternal entity that comes from elsewhere: the entity who lives a thousand lives, who has a thousand faces and a thousand parents.

The late Alfred Tomatis, an ear, nose and throat specialist at the Paris School of Medicine, concluded after 25 years of research that hearing precedes all forms of cellular organization, as if the whole creative process depended on it. This idea—revolutionary in the eyes of modern science—merely confirms what the Vedic texts put forward several thousands years ago. Tomatis showed how quick the fetus is to develop the ear. Why? Simply because life *is* listening.

Tomatis' discoveries led him to design an "electronic ear," which he used in the treatment of psychotic children. The device helps children artificially return to the reassuring environment of the womb, filtering their mother's voice and making it sound as it did to the fetus still in the uterus.

The scientist, with proof in hand, arrives a little late. By the time laboratory results have been recorded, the life-giving process is already well under way. From the dawn of time, mothers have known that the fetus has the ability of perception. As Professor Tomatis remarked, "What any mother is able to teach us—that her child moves in the womb when it perceives music, a sound or a voice—is viewed as a genuine revelation in certain scientific quarters."[41]

Tomatis' research proved, however, to what extent the act of listening is ontogenetically rooted in every human being's deepest self. The mother and father should be fully aware of this fact if they are to help their child develop the desire to listen, to live, to be free and to love. For listening, it should be recalled, is primarily opening one's heart or, according to Tomatis, "entering into understanding and loving communion with another being."[42] Hence, listening alone is a form of communication in the broadest and noblest sense.

In speaking to their as yet unborn child, the mother and father should speak to the eternal entity that comes from elsewhere: the entity who lives a thousand lives, who has a thousand faces and a thousand parents. It is with this entity that they should converse. They will find the words of sufficient strength, the songs of love, the creative and assertive words that will cause the immortal soul—which has found shelter in the mother's womb and whom the parents already call their child—to vibrate.

From within, the knowing mother hears the praises sung by the atoms of existence and responds to them with the silent song of love. The being she bears within her is the rhythm, and she is the time. In this unmasked state, life is revealed to her through hearing; what she perceives cannot be dismissed as the interaction of chemical substances. Indeed, what she perceives of life is a "certain something" which cannot be destroyed, which permeates her entire body, which is immeasurable, which knows neither life nor death and which will never cease to exist. Unborn, immortal, primordial and eternal, this "certain something" has no beginning and will have no end.

This phenomenon, present as a fetus, is attentive to its mother's love. It is this "certain something" that the Bible praises and which speaks to the Creator in these terms: "Thine eyes did see my substance, yet being imperfect; and in thy book all my members were written, which in continuance were fashioned, when as yet there was none of them."[43]

We are asked to put aside our misconceptions about life in the womb and acknowledge that the fetus not only hears, but it listens. It listens, intuitively understands, and grasps. This truth, demonstrated by Vedic as well as modern science, still has far to go before being generally accepted. But the advent of this new cycle in consciousness brings with it an immediate and intimate understanding of what it is to listen. This heightened sense of awareness is about to shift the accepted paradigm. By developing this consciousness, we embrace life; we understand that embedded in each sound that reaches us is a message from the Absolute. To listen profoundly, there is no need for an outer ear. It is but the heart's perception of the invisible world, the soul-to-soul dialogue.

This sublime communication is revealed in the Sufi tradition of Master Qushari. In his short treatise on the *sana*, or esoteric hearing, he writes: "Spiritual hearing is the understanding of hidden things by listening to hearts, by discerning realities which are the object of our quest and which comprise the signs of the divine present in all creatures."

THe new CHILDRen

In communicating with the fetus, and indeed in all communication, we must realize that the words of everyday language are absolutely devoid of meaning to the soul, for it perceives all that goes beyond words. It is the intentionally generated energy, the affectionate warmth carried through a pleasant, soft, loving and compassionate voice that the soul feels. Like the swan of Greek mythology that has the power to separate water from milk, the living being draws love from sound. Beyond the fetus and beyond the dialogue of humans is the sublime center that transcends all science; it is capable of hearing

the music of our souls, in spite of the endless commotion of our mundane thoughts and words.

Before the beginning there was listening, declared Tomatis, adding, "Human vitality is based solely on the function of listening."[44] Now the goal of this auditory contemplation consists of obeying life as it manifests genetically. Knowing how to obey the rules of life gives us the hope of one day escaping the laws set by humankind: the impermanent laws that lead us blindly from bad to worse, toward a risky, dangerous and uncertain future as long as they remain separate from universal laws.

Listening to life will enable us to perceive universal principles: compassion, purity, truthfulness and sobriety. It will lead us toward an age of mastery. The mastery of the art of profound listening will be the greatest accomplishment of human evolution. It will provide the genuine riches that confer on human beings a state of divine freedom, autonomy and total self-satisfaction. New parents, aware of the paramount importance of noise, sound, song and words in their child's development during gestation, will give birth to a new generation, much more advanced than the generations that created the painful industrial and technological worlds. Nourished with loving and beautiful sound vibrations from conception, these new children will usher in a new age on Earth.

THE POWER OF WORDS

IN THE BEGINNING WAS SONG...

In principium erat verbum: This sentence can be found in the first line of the first paragraph of the Gospel according to Saint John. Various exegetes have given it numerous meanings, but in general the sentence is translated as: "In the beginning was the Word." Some translators are of the opinion, however, that *verbum* could mean "sound or song." Therefore it could be said that sound, song, words or speech are brought forth from the same energy. If in the beginning was the word, or the sound, and if the sound was the Divine Principle—as the Gospel states—then its inherent energy must be all-powerful because it is the primeval creative energy. In this sense, the Biblical scriptures echo the Vedic scriptures, the latter stating: "In the beginning was Brahman [the impersonal aspect of the Absolute] with whom was the word, and the word is Brahman."

Although religions are often divided by trivial disagreements over terminology, these two statements reflect an important parallel between Hinduism and Christianity. The word, the primeval cosmic sound, can be found everywhere, from the Hebrews to the Tibetans, from Islam to Buddhism. The God-sound is omnipresent in humanity's history and is always closely linked to the essence of consciousness. It is found in the Kabbala and in all great cultures. *Om, aum, amn, ameen, omon, omen, yahuvah:* The list of names for the God-sound is endless. It is the Logos, the famous lost word of esoteric traditions. Krishna says in the *Mahabharat,* "I am the sound of ether." Saint John, in the first chapter of the King James Bible, states, "In the beginning was the Word and the Word was with God, and the Word was God. The same was in the beginning with God. All things were made by Him, and without Him was not any thing made that was made. In Him was life, and the life was the light of men. And the light shineth in darkness, and the darkness comprehended it not."

According to the original Aramaean text, "in the beginning" implies an eternal state prior to all creation. "Word" comes from the Latin *verbum,* which was derived from the Greek *logos,* that is to say, "the word." *Logos* was commonly used in Greek philosophy to designate the Divine Intelligence, or the organizer of the world. According to Emile Osty, a renowned linguistic expert, by *verbum,* Saint John means "the substantial and eternal word."[45]

Victor Hugo, one of the fathers of French literature, declared: "And the word, we should recognize, is a living entity." The word is alive. It is a gift from the powers beyond. When we say, "I am," we call upon a divine power and, gradually, the qualities of the assertions that follow that phrase tend to manifest within us. It is quite obvious that the pumpkin does not change into a coach overnight, but the assertion sets in motion the process through which the word takes form in matter. After several repetitions of the sentence, "I am in good health," you will likely feel a sensation of genuine well-being throughout your body. Try the experiment yourself! In turn, this sensation or emotion will set in motion the phenomenon of health.

It is astonishing to observe and realize that this process is effective whether the assertions are made in a state of awareness or not. It is imperative that we understand that we typically use the tremendous power of words in a totally unconscious and negative way, which is one of humankind's tragedies.

The Creator has given humans an unlimited power, that of the spoken word. Though this power is neutral in itself, its use can produce opposite effects. The word can constitute the source of our happiness or of our misery. Over a one-week period, should we repeat the assertion, "I am seriously ill"—especially before going to sleep—in all likelihood our body will weaken and a serious illness will develop. If we are sick and repeat each day, "I am perfectly healed," we will heal if we can conceive of a perfect state of health within us.

THE INVISIBLE BRIDGES OF HARMONIC RESONANCE

For a long time, we humans believed that our primary faculty was the will. Through his research and thousands of healings, Émile Coué, who revolutionized psychological automatism and shed great light on the far-reaching field of autosuggestion, proved that it is not the will that is the primary human faculty, but the imagination.[46] The imagination has a direct effect on the individual. This faculty is independent from and stronger than the will. "Imagine" that you are relaxed and your muscles will immediately slacken, your nervous tension abate. "Will" yourself to be relaxed and you will become increasingly tense.

The word acts directly on the imagination. When human beings become aware of the power within them, they regain mastery of their lives and become worthy of their celestial origins. This power could be called autosuggestion, suggestion, or the power of the subconscious, among other terms. What we call it is of little importance. This power has always existed and will always exist. As the holders of this force, we have the right and the duty to develop it and to use it in a beneficial sense.

All this can be explained in a very simple manner, by borrowing data from the field of micro-vibratory physics. According to Hermes' Law, nothing is inert; all vibrates, all is vibration. For example, if object A vibrates at a frequency of 4,000 cycles per second and object B vibrates at a frequency of 10,000 cycles per second, then objects A and B are not vibrating in harmony. They are not harmonious; they are not attuned to the same frequency. To harmonize them, that is to say, to put them in tune with each other, it is necessary to make them vibrate at the same speed. Similarly, two persons who do not have similar desires, or who have not reached similar intellectual or intuitive conclusions, will not vibrate at the same frequency and will therefore be antipathetic to one another.

> The imagination has a direct effect on the individual. This faculty is independent from and stronger than the will.

When human beings think or use their power of imagination and assertion, they begin to vibrate at the same frequency as the frequency they visualize. This is the phenomenon of vibratory responsiveness.

What is absolutely extraordinary is to realize that by naming an object with a spoken word, we become perfectly attuned to that object's frequency and we literally enter into contact with it. Everyone knows that the medium of sound is vibratory. Through the simple action of naming an object and thinking and concentrating on it, imagining all its details, shape, color, qualities and attributes that are particular to it, the brain projects an impulse toward the object. The sound vibration that designates it represents its "counterpart." Therefore, words and names are "supports" or "witnesses" between creative imagination and the object itself.

For instance, when the imagination—through the intermediary of the mental computer that is the brain—seeks to attune itself to the harmony frequency, the word becomes the vibratory relay between the brain and the state of perfect harmony. In other words, this sound becomes the connection between the archetype and the human being. It makes possible direct contact with the unlimited energies of cosmic harmony, which have existed throughout eternity within ourselves and allow us to feel its vibrations. Thus, the word's frequency—the number of sound vibrations it is composed of—builds a bridge no less real because it is invisible, between us and any given major current of cosmic energy.

At this level, it is not necessary to reason in order to understand, but rather to experiment so as to feel and realize. Jean-Jacques Rousseau, one of the greatest philosophers of the Enlightenment, had a deep understanding of this basic point when he wrote: "When man starts to reason, he ceases to feel."

The waves of universal harmony can be picked up if careful attention is brought to this investigation. These waves then permeate the living being's subtle molecular structure and entirely modify the living being. The sound of the spoken word links the word to the archetype to which it refers. The word is nothing other than the name by which an object, a form of energy, an element or a person is designated. The great archetypal vibrations are always available in the cosmos, and it is sufficient to attune us to their respective currents to reap their benefits. This "alliance" is forged with the help of both the spoken word and the imagination. Thus, the fundamental frequencies of health, beauty, strength, knowledge, richness and so forth exist in the universe and are constantly available to those who wish to benefit from their vibrations. The vibrations of anger, fear, anxiety, poverty and greed are also available, however.

The spoken word is a double-edged sword. It is up to human beings to develop some discrimination in order to have the opportunity to choose, in full knowledge of the facts, the particular energy they wish to tap. The old saying, "Turn your tongue seven times before speaking," reflects the truth of the power of words.

Precious vibrations and powerful energies exist in the spoken word. They are astonishing to feel and to put into action. When we are aware of the power of our words, we become captain of the vessel of the body-spirit in which the soul travels. The sublime responsibility for our own consciousness is proof of humans' existential autonomy and prohibits all claims that an exterior "master" is responsible, as is so often done in Western religious systems and sometimes even in those of the East out of sheer ignorance of the cosmic laws. The soul is the only cause of all that happens to it. By what means? Through the simple and terrible tool that is the word.

As one old saying goes: "If man digs his grave with his fork, he also forges his destiny with his tongue." The Bible tells us that what comes out of our mouths matters. Each word, each expression we utter, determines a little more the circumstances that will crystallize in our lives. What is tragic, and at the same time somewhat miraculous, is the absolute nature of the process. It takes place when the words are pronounced unconsciously or automatically or even jokingly. Like a computer, the subconscious registers data without having the slightest sense of humor.

> We typically use the tremendous power of words in a totally unconscious and negative way, which is one of humankind's tragedies.

The same type of energetic fusion happens with both positive and negative affirmations. Unfortunately, the result is often much more evident in the negative affirmation, since the spoken word in those cases is typically uttered absentmindedly, unconsciously, automatically and without the slightest effort. Under these conditions, the energetic fusion takes place much more easily.

The assertion bears within it the power of wishes, promises and decrees. Luck does not exist. When we affirm, "I am really lucky," everything happens at matter's subtle level, as if we had made a pact with luck itself. Karl Otto Schmidt, the great master of dynamic psychology, has irrefutably established this reality and has taught people to employ it to benefit all aspects of life. According to him, by human beings' power to determine what they will become, they become it. In this way, humans are the undeniable masters and primeval causes of the circumstances and events that mark the entire course of their existence. Their lives are in their own hands. For this reason, in Sanskrit the human being is called *prabhu*, or master.

According to Dr. Schmidt:

> When you say, "I am," your thoughts are all ears because every "I am" is a call to accomplishment. Every thought related to an "I am" manifests an increasing tendency to accomplish and mobilizes the forces of growth or penury, failure or happiness. So that good alone manifests itself in your life, be careful that all sentences starting with "I am" are directed toward positive goals. "I am sick, I am unhappy, I am tired, I am persecuted by destiny, I am poor, I am suffering, I am weak, I am in misery"; all are clear orders given to the powers of life to create the corresponding states or to develop them more deeply. If, on the contrary, you consciously say: "I am free, I am strong, I am contented, I am always on top, I am fate's favorite, I am rich in successes, I am at one with the forces of good, I am conscious of God, I am destiny's ally, I am rich," then more and more these assertions will come to hold true. "I am" signifies: I am spirit born of the Divinity's spirit; I am a universal child and life's plenitude is mine in my own right. "I am," such is the name of the divine in you. Each time you express it consciously, you speak as God speaks, saying: "Let it be" to all that you assert.[47]

THE SPELL-LIKE SONG
OF OUR DAILY SPEECH

Attempting to solve a complex problem without the benefit of contemplation is a hopeless endeavor. Those whom begin from a spiritual foundation, however, will meet with sure and solid success.

The type of planning we're used to doing on a daily basis may undoubtedly provide immediate benefits, and these apparent gains often seem undeniable. According to the laws of life, however, what is acquired from the world of matter is temporal, and thus, ultimately unfulfilling. The only lasting success stems from inner activity—from the realm of the spirit.

Within us lies the root of all sound images projected on the giant screen of our own existence. Peaceful souls do not seek situations of conflict. The harmony we spread around ourselves when our souls are in peace constitutes the most effective type of protection against encounters with feelings contrary to harmony.

Once the Earth is inhabited by such souls, conflicts of interest and great international passions will completely disappear from the face of the planet because they will no longer be nourished by the cacophony, dissonance and disharmony of thoughts. Nations will no longer disagree because they will vibrate in unison to a common note: the taste for real happiness. This superior taste, the genuine music of the soul, will be characteristic of the present age. The taste for the vain sacrifice that marked the preceding age—the sacrifice of man's spirituality in exchange for industrialization—has already weakened. Though this sacrifice may have been necessary to build the foundations of a new age, it no longer serves us.

Today, it has become crucial and urgent to realize that this age, expected for millennia, will not manifest without the practice of the mastery of thoughts. In a way, thoughts are the reflexes of the subconscious; the only way to program the subconscious is to be "conscious of the conscious," to register or store consciously precise thoughts in the electromagnetic fields (or mnemonic engrams) of the subconscious.

To do so, we have at our disposal a precious, extraordinary tool, a genuine gift from heaven: the spell-like song of our daily speech. All those who accomplish great things, and all those who achieve true success, put their mental and verbal activities in the service of their ideals. How is this done? By recording in the mental process a thought that is precise, persevering, sustained and continuously nourished by the dynamic life-giving force of assertive words. This is in keeping with yoga techniques aimed at mental mastery, in which the repetition of certain series of sounds, all related to the control of breathing, are crucial.

The efficiency of these ancient methods is well established. In a sense, our daily conversations are a type of chanting; these spoken words, particularly assertions, act upon consciousness. In turn, the latter influences the subconscious, which, through programmed reflexes, produces the thought. The thought itself is the creator of destiny. To paraphrase Saint Germain, we allow what we think and feel to take on a physical form. We arrive where our thoughts and words take us, becoming our meditation, so to speak. At one extreme is the word produced by, and held within, the thought; at the other extreme is destiny. In this sense, we can understand how the word represents the divine power *par excellence* and the human being, its heir, a potential god. This is not to say that man is God, as is the habit in popular esoteric circles. At the risk of creating displeasure, I maintain that the universal soul and the distinct soul never lose their spiritual and absolute individuality. The oldest book in creation, the *Brahma Samhita,* said to have been written by Brahma himself, has much to say on this topic, notably that it is possible to blend into the energetic impersonal Brahman light, but this pseudo-annihilation proves to be yet another illusion. According to these writings, true liberation lies in the love relationship that develops between the individual spirit soul (*jiva*) and the divine personality, the one who is called by a thousand different names and worshiped in a thousand different forms. Nonetheless it is the same one; it is the one who has always awaited us.

An entire range of limitless relationships *(rasas)* can arise from this loving and mystical exchange. The masters of universal devotion have identified five great families of *rasas* (neutral, respectful, friendly, parental and conjugal). I cannot elaborate on this topic without moving beyond the limits of this work. Readers wishing to learn more should refer to the books that deal with the subject of divine love, in particular the spiritual classic by an unknown author, *The Imitation of Jesus Christ,* and *The Nectar of Devotion* by Rupa Goswami.

If living beings are God, but have "forgotten" they are, as some like to claim, then which God are we referring to? How can God, who is omniscient by definition, forget anything? Mere common sense leads us to reject this inconsistency. Living beings are not God. We are of divine essence, however, and participate in the Abso-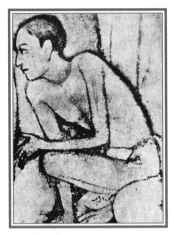 lute: we have its qualities, its attributes and its powers, but only in infinitesimal quantity. Which, on the human scale, is phenomenal when we imagine the limitless powers of the Absolute.

Humans are of divine nature. We hold within our souls and on our lips the sound keys of our own destiny and that of the world. Through our assertions, we have the power to create the universe we desire. Coming from a "Heavenly Father," what could be more liberal?

LISTENING TO THE HIGHER CONSCIOUSNESS: MANTRAESTHETICS

The nations who will successfully achieve the great harmony of the age of happiness will be those who play the music of their soul on the harp that is their language. Awareness of the spoken word—the song of destiny—constitutes the next step in humanity's evolution. The conscious affir-

mative word is a high-voltage regenerator and reharmo-
nizer for material and subtle bodies—an inexhaustible
source of strength for the physical and psychic natures. It
constitutes the foundation of global health. It stimulates
the fire of digestion and the organs' proper functioning.
The brief sentence, "I am in perfect health," repeated in
the serenity of the morning and in the tranquility of the
evening, with the knowledge that what the new human
decrees is already making its way toward us, can provide
more well-being than any chemical product. Trying it is
enough to convince you!

In the near future, when the healing power of sound
will be better known, it will not be surprising to read at
the bottom of a prescription the following note: Medication should be taken with psycho-acoustic vibration—"I
feel perfectly well, I am in excellent health"—to be repeated ten times a day, morning, noon and evening.

In the late 19th century, Émile Coué treated, relieved
and healed thousands of patients considered incurable
by the school of medicine of the time. His treatment con-
sisted of the repetition of a simple sentence: "Every day,
in every way, I am getting better and better." Coué understood the close relationship that exists between the vibratory energies of the word and psychological activity.
In his view, suggestion only acts when it has been transformed into autosuggestion, in other words, when it has
been accepted.

What, then, ought we to accept? The verb "to suggest" comes from the Latin *suggerere,* which exactly sig-
nifies "to bear under." It is precisely this still mysterious
force, hidden in the sound of words, held by the affirma-
tive spoken word, that it is necessary to accept (the verb

"to accept" comes from the Latin *acceptare*, which means "to receive"). What is accepted (received) becomes accessible. From this point on, autosuggestion can be used effectively to achieve therapeutic ends.

Like electricity, sound is a neutral energy; it can be either beneficial or malevolent. Everything depends on how it is used. Generally, we are masters at practicing harmful autosuggestion, without ever having taken lessons. Why does negative suggestion succeed so well? Because, it bears repeating, we practice it unconsciously and effortlessly. Some people automatically state: "I know that I will never succeed" or "I know that [this or that] catastrophe, [this or that] obstacle is insurmountable, unavoidable." They make these assertions without any particular effort, which means that these words, and the power they hold, penetrate easily into the subconscious, which accepts them. And because the latter regulates the functioning of our physical, psychic or moral being, it causes everything to happen in accordance with the order it has received.

> We hold within our souls and on our lips the sound keys of our own destiny and that of the world. Through our assertions, we have the power to create the universe we desire.

Persistent, but not rigid, repetition of a sound vibration contained in a positive sound-word can reverse the negatively programmed subconscious and induce its creative mechanism to work not only in a positive sense, but also toward higher states of consciousness.

In future years, this idea will be at the origins of a new science that will synthesize, on the one hand, sound forces (music, speech, subliminal noises) and the power of autosuggestion and, on the other hand, the purifying effect of inspired meditative song. This new science could be called "mantraesthetics" (from the Sanskrit *manatatra*, or liberating tool, and from the Greek *aisthesie*, or feeling). This system of knowledge will have as its objective sensitizing the human subconscious to the sound vibrations in the spoken words that free the mind from itself.

There already exists a Bulgarian method of accelerated training known as suggestology that uses music and rhythmic breathing to activate the brain's right hemisphere. But for the most part, autosuggestive methodologies are used to achieve goals related to the body and the conscious mind. Mantraesthetics will be directed toward modifying consciousness and awakening the soul.

To grasp the scope and effectiveness of such an approach, it is necessary to define the various roles played by the conscious, the subconscious and the unconscious, or *supraconscious*. The word "unconscious" is generally used to designate all that is beyond the conscious, or "supraconscious."

The conscious mind always tries to analyze things logically. Unfortunately, this quality often allows it to block the intuitive information that comes from the deepest part of us. These profound intuitive perceptions stem from the supraconscious and are relayed by the subconscious.

We should not allow ourselves to be intimidated by these intellectual sounding words, which the authors of scientific works are all too fond of using. In reality, these concepts are simple. To understand the close relationship between these three elements, one need only imagine that the subconscious is a letter carrier whose work is to transmit letters (messages) from the central post office (the supraconscious) to the home mailbox (the conscious).

The subconscious, as an intermediary, creates a bridge between the supraconscious and the conscious. It is an intuitive half-consciousness. By the proper use of sounds, the practice of mantraesthetics provokes such a state of relaxation that the subconscious has no other choice but to allow the supraconscious to relay information through it. Thus, these "revelations" seep into the conscious.

In fact, in certain states of relaxation or meditation, the inferior ego is in a condition of passivity. This is when the doors of the inner supraconscious open. All sound perceptions, words, names, assertions, remarks and so forth accumulate in the supraconscious. This data is collected and encoded without any real awareness on our part. Multiple sounds, conversations and pieces of music are stored inside the supraconscious, which could be compared to a magnetic band on which, among other things, is recorded all that the ear perceives in this life in addition to a portion of what it has previously perceived.

In a sense, the supraconscious is an accumulator of images, sounds, emotions and memories directly connected to the manner in which we allow ourselves to perceive existence. The instant the individual's life force is separated from the chemical elements that comprise its carnal form (a transition falsely called "death"), this accumulation of thoughts, desires and supraconscious memories determines the conditions in which the soul will reincarnate. Therefore, pre-embryonic life (or anterior life) is simply a preparation for the present life, and the present life is the workshop in which are built the predispositions of all future life.

Seen from this angle, mantraesthetics could potentially have unimaginable consequences on human evolution, providing humankind with access to the supraconscious memories carried from rebirth to rebirth. In order to perceive the song of the supraconscious, it is keenly recommended that one enter a state favorable to the free circulation of energies between the supraconscious and the conscious. The role of subliminal and relaxing music and above all, of listening to inspired meditative songs, can then prove to be of precious assistance. Indeed, the main quality of these songs is precisely to break down the barriers that rise between the "post office" (the supraconscious), the "letter carrier" (the subconscious) and the "home mailbox" (the conscious).

Once these obstacles are obliterated, it is then possible for energies seeking only to circulate, to flow freely, imparting throughout the entire being an equilibrium never achieved before. From this perfect equilibrium are born new sensations, such as invincible joy, serenity in the face of affliction, absolute trust in one's self and heightened perception of a universal intelligence.

In the mantraesthetic technique, the human being becomes a sensitive organ. What only the ear ordinarily feels spreads through the entire person and naturally becomes movement. The assimilated experience becomes dance, song, laughter, tears of joy and, eventually, a global absorption into the realm of ecstasy. This ecstatic state is provoked by the perception of the inalterability of the soul and by the awareness of the immortal love relationship that unites this soul to the primeval essence.

another evolution

For the conscious, the sound of the word, the spoken word, is a symbol. What is this symbol? It is the idea expressed by a particular sound. The name of an object holds within it all the symbolic elements that are at the origin of the existence of the object it represents. This is why the sages of all eras and traditions have reached the same conclusion for millennia: the world is music; the universe and all of creation are sound vibration.

When all cells within the cosmos vibrate in harmony, free from egotistic or anarchic desires and focused only on the will of their creator, an immense cosmic symphony will be heard in all planes of existence and living beings everywhere will once again find the eternal rhythm of love, the celestial melody of the music of the soul. Such is the goal of evolution.

The soul embodies the reality of the manifestation that appears to the eyes of the physical body in one form or another. The soul is the idea held within the symbol's form. It is the substance, and the ephemeral forms it takes through the nature of its desires constitute only various shadows of this substance. The melody never comes after the harmony, but the inverse. In the same manner, it is not the substance that comes after the shape, but the inverse. Since everything in creation tends to follow this pattern, the idea's manifestation tends to follow automatically its symbolized expression in the sound formula. This is why a state of peace occurs *around* the word "peace," a state of health crystallizes *around* the word "health," and a climate of violence is felt where words symbolizing violence are frequently spoken. Success comes after the word "success," and wealth appears where the sentence "I am rich" is often repeated, and so forth.

In the esoteric tradition, the deity manifests itself and appears under the particular shape invoked by the musical energies contained in its multiple names. A thousand different names will eventually result in a thousand different apparitions, whether personified or not. However, all manifestations are manifestations of the same substance. If we take into account the physiological effects inherent in the emission of a given syllable, we realize that, through speech, through the sung statement, words are taken charge of by those who pronounce them. We take possession of them and enter into a vibratory union with them, physically and psychically.

As the idea is confined within the sound symbol of the word, so is the soul imprisoned in the body. The spoken word is an idea in the making, ready to manifest itself in a given form, that is to say, to be materially formulated. This is what is normally called evolution, which is generally accompanied by the strange impression that evolution is the result of genetic mutation. Nothing is further from reality!

There is an evolution, but it is not biological. A monkey does not become a human through genetic mutation. Rather, the life force animating the monkey's body may reincarnate in a human form. The teachings that could have helped us understand this are absent from the Bible. The Catholic Church suppressed them. In the year 553 A.D., during the second Council of Constantinople, the thirst for power pushed Byzantine Emperor Justinian to suppress all teachings concerning reincarnation from Christian scriptures. Nonetheless the majority in the West still accept the idea, or they reject the Bible without trying to understand it.

It is not the body that evolves, but the soul that inhabits it, through transmigration from one body to another. A musician can wish to play on a more advanced instrument. It is the musician who changes instruments, however, not the instrument that changes musicians.

By basing his theory of the evolution of species on the premise that a genuine genetic variation takes place from generation to generation, Darwin—and following in his footsteps, industrial civilization as a whole—rejected the archetype or the specific  essence Plato referred to as *eidos*. It is  this *eidos* that is found in the sound of the word that symbolically represents something. It is the *eidos* that evolves through the forms it takes on, through the forms material nature agrees to lend it. Evolution does indeed occur, but not as Darwin understood it.

Paradoxically, Darwin's hypothesis identifies a plan in nature, but does not inquire as to whom the planner is, which is absurd. As soon as one recognizes the existence of a plan, one must also acknowledge a creator, architect or designer. And if we claim that the great harmony of nature simply functions mechanically, should we not recognize that, of necessity, there must exist an intelligent mechanical energy produced by a mechanic who makes it work?

Visionaries call this primeval energy the Great Spirit, God, the soul of the universe. Scientific intellectuals refer to it as the Great Unifying Theory. Beyond these two visions, one reality exists. Elevated and purified humankind waits in the silence of the eternal.

Behind the immense symphony of nature is the intelligence of a divine composer. To hear and interpret the music of the soul is to follow this creator's directives for perfection. This direction is precisely given through the creative word, the word that was in the beginning and by which all has been created. Humans' spoken words have the power to symbolize the evolutionary idea of divinity. Here, the verb "to symbolize" is taken in its classical sense, which means, "to agree with." This agreement will enable us to rediscover the therapeutic qualities of speech.

> As soon as one recognizes the existence of a plan, one must also acknowledge a creator, architect or designer.

The various physical aspects of the living being are neither a product of chance, nor the fruit of a hypothetical genetic mutation. They represent material nature's exact response to the desires of human beings. Through its own free will, the soul chooses to listen to a particular type of music and to pronounce certain words. Thus, it decides the circumstances and events of its evolution. By continuously surrounding itself with elevated sound vibrations, it creates the body of light it will inhabit in its future existence. By consciously immersing itself in an atmosphere charged with frequencies from the hearing and chanting of unlimited names related to the Absolute, the soul rediscovers the memory of its foundation and finds within itself (and not in the politics and bureaucracies of any exterior religion) the strength to travel through the higher stages of its cosmic fulfillment.

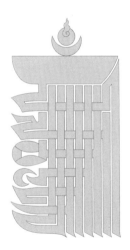

THE HIGHEST PREMONITION

Mantras can be thought of as tools that liberate the mind. They are not "magic formulas" whose function is to transcend cosmic laws or hypnotize the entity that chants or recites them. The goal of mantras is to awaken the life forces that exist in the human soul and have existed throughout eternity. The Sanskrit word *mantra* means "mental liberation." This sound, or combination of sounds, delivers the mind from its worldly conditioning and limitations.

Lama Anagarika Govinda defines mantras as "archetypal sounds and verbal symbols that have their origin in the very structure of our consciousness. Thus, they are not arbitrary creations springing from an individual initiative; they are born from the collective or general human experience, modified only by cultural or religious traditions."[48]

A mantra is therefore a symbol. According to Carl Jung, it is an idea that corresponds to the conscious being's highest premonition. This highest premonition is the awareness of our divine nature. This awareness is complete when it includes the consciousness of the Absolute within us and its unifying relationship with us. This union of devotion and love represents the quintessence of absolute happiness. The ultimate goal of the practice of mantras is precisely to recover this lost divine relationship.

Mantras are found in all cultures, traditions and religious systems. They are not exclusive to the Eastern world. Certain litanies from original Christianity are also mantras. Muslims, Buddhists and Zoroastrians have their specific mantras as well.

In Western society, which is primarily informed by Judeo-Christian tradition, many people feel more in harmony with Christian "mantric" methods, which are more closely related to their culture. This is fine, as it is important to feel at ease with the mantras we use. The mantra itself matters little provided we reach the ecstasy of spiritual deliverance, a mystical ecstasy that the sound vibration will undoubtedly trigger from the depths of any serious practitioner.

There are, of course, thousands of mantras with different functions from this relational goal. These mantras can serve to reach all kinds of goals that are more or less linked to material energy. The genuine goal of practicing mantras, however, is to connect oneself to the Divine. The process that leads to awareness of this relationship is not an upward process, but a downward one. In other words, these things are not born of a reflection in which the consciousness attempts to reach a spiritual level through intellectual effort. On the contrary, this awareness is a state of grace springing up from the depths of the heart.

This state is offered, with no underlying motivation, by the medium of a master-guide. The mantric tradition is oral. The *shakti,* the energy, is passed from mouth to ear, from master to disciple. To receive a mantra from an authentic living master is, in itself, an initiation. This initiatory experience is a necessity for whoever wishes to follow the mantra's path, and it represents the beginning of its practice (*sadhana*).

> The mantra itself matters little provided we reach the ecstasy of spiritual deliverance, a mystical ecstasy that the sound vibration will undoubtedly trigger from the depths of any serious practitioner.

The mantra's symbolic sound forms a bridge between superficial consciousness and the essential ego located on the incorporeal level. On this plane, the structures of language as we know them disappear to make room for pure emotions and feelings that are impossible to express through verbal concepts. For this reason, most mantric formulas incorporate primary sounds without any precise meaning and which do not express any concept or idea. These are root sounds or seed syllables (*bija*). These root sounds trigger the awakening of superior emotions by directly influencing the consciousness with vibrations whose resonances predate all human language.

In Tibetan mysticism, for example, we find the sound *hūṁ,* which represents individuality and induces the descent from the state of universality to the depths of the human soul. The *u* is pronounced as it is in the English language. The stroke above the *u* extends the sound; the dot above the *m* indicates the mantric nature of the sound seed and is said to turn back the sound toward the interior. The exterior vibration we hear is therefore transferred to the inaudible, but real, inner frequency. It is unnecessary to think about this or to try to reason it out. Similarly, when music or a song moves us, we can-

not really explain why. We simply feel something particularly powerful moving and evolving within us. We feel
acutely that this energy moves the mountains of our indifference and insensitivity.

Exactly the same thing occurs with the seed sound
(bija) of a mantra. The inner frequency of the phonic
group of letters, inaudible to the physical ear, holds the
all-powerful energy known as the *shabda.* Without the
perception of the *shabda,* or mystical sound enclosed
in the mantra, which the initiate seeks to discover, the
mantra's power cannot manifest fully.

The sound *om* is the supreme
bija. As the *hūṁ* is the descent
of God toward the soul, *om* is the
opening of the soul to God as it
corresponds to the ascent of individuality toward universality,
toward the infinite. On this sub-
ject, the *Srimad Bhagavatam* says: "The sacred syllable
om, vested with unsuspected powers, blooms like a lotus
within the pure soul. It represents the Absolute Truth in
its three aspects: impersonal reality, the Supreme Soul
and the Supreme Being. All the Vedic resonances emanate
from the sound *om,* which is begotten in the soul."[49]

Countless pages have been written on the meaning
and tenor of the sound *om*; it's beneficial to read and assimilate them. It is even more extraordinary, however, to
experience the power of *om* directly.

In a comfortable position, relax your body by breathing deeply. Once you are calm, pronounce the sacred mantra without attempting to understand it, but merely by
trying, with a simple heart, to feel its exceptional frequen-

cies. In time, all metaphysical explanations fade into the background as the unsuspected realm of mystical experience is approached. This is sound, vibrant with joy and pregnant with love. The heart expands under radiating warmth. The mind that, a few minutes before, spun painfully in all directions is focused in a single direction, concentrated on a point located at the center of the heart. A ray of peace emanates from this point. Body and spirit are spontaneously bathed in an immense sense of gratitude. As we continue to chant, we realize the power of the mantra and the stunning immensity of transcendental regions. Once awakened, the individual emerges from his or her old shell and vibrates in harmony with the silent peace in which it is possible to perceive the sublime voice of his soul. When this hour finally comes for us, we recognize our origin as stemming from the Absolute. We remember that physical life is but a theatre performance. From this point on, we no longer fear anything.

PROFOUNDLY LISTENING TO THE REVEALED WORD

While the repetition of a given sound architecture can provide well-being, fortune, health and all types of things, as noted, the ultimate goal of mantra practice is to help us rediscover our spiritual identity. Through this awareness, we can reestablish the unique relationship that unites us to the living light of God. This rediscovery of the soul's life develops from listening. Those who lend an attentive ear to mantric sound vibrations rapidly rid their hearts of all impurity. The importance of listening is mentioned on several occasions in the revealed scriptures. In the *Garuda Purana,* the Vedic scriptures eloquently advocate the practice of listening: "Existence conditioned by the universe of matter can be compared to the state of a man who lies unconscious, the victim of a snake's bite. The vibrations of a mantra can dissipate both these two forms of unconsciousness."

There are indeed given mantras capable of restoring life to someone who seems already dead from the serpent's bite and someone who, plunged into deep unconsciousness, remains in a type of comatose state. There are specific mantras capable of annihilating the venom's effects. In the comatose state, as in the state of deep sleep, the ear is the only sensory organ still active; someone who seems already dead can still hear the sound that will save his or her life. In another kind of coma, ignorance of the soul's existence has plunged humanity into the deep sleep of indifference and insensitivity, a result of crass materialism. In the coma of illusion, the exchange of love between the individual spirit soul and the sweet Absolute has been replaced by a pitiable sense of impersonalism. In this state, nihilism and existentialism block the descent of great energies of light and peace that are always ready to inundate the world. This is why sages perceive humanity as a transitory sphere plunged in the deepest darkness of ignorance, envy and hatred. Under the illusion of restrictive egoism, humans seem dead, though they vainly turn in all directions in search of a happiness that continues to elude them.

This lack of well-being can be healed by profoundly

listening to all that is related to absolute truth. According to *Srimad Bhagavatam* (2.1.5), this is what is recommended in the *Vedanta Sutra:* "He who wishes to be freed from all suffering, should hear what is related to God, should praise Him and keep in mind his personal aspect, Him, the Supreme Soul, the master and redeemer of all suffering."

The fire of inner life is thereby lit, and the living beings, having been plunged in a state of unconsciousness by the anxieties of their limited existence, come out of their chronic lethargy and awaken in the world of their own divinity. The author of the Vedic scriptures, Vyasadev, describes the importance of listening to revealed scriptures as they have been given to humans through the words of countless masters of  truth: "It is essential to lend an attentive ear to the chants and sayings of the *acharyas* [spiritual lineage holders], which flow like rivers of nectar from their lunar-like faces." The soul which wholeheartedly listens to these spiritual sounds will undoubtedly see itself freed from hunger, thirst, fear and affliction and from all illusion related to the reductionist material consciousness.

It is indeed through this consciousness of poverty, in opposition to the consciousness of all-powerful plenitude, that most illnesses are born—illnesses that first eat away at the spirit, and then the body.

FREEDOM FROM FEAR

Fear and anxiety, founded and unfounded, are rampant in the minds and hearts of human beings. Due to this all sorts of negative thoughts are hatched. These are the chaotic factors underlying the psychological disorders suffered by humankind. Many illnesses treated by doctors originate in both the body and the mind, and are thus psychosomatic in nature. When those who practice conventional medicine move beyond experimentation on animals and physio-chemical laws, they will discover the science of autosuggestion.

Conscious or unconscious listening to the materially polluted sounds that saturate the modern world creates an overall autosuggestion of danger, destitution and violence. Thus influenced, we are subconsciously hypnotized by fear, and life becomes a narrow space, minimized by an existential anguish based on a profound lack of intuitive knowledge. While this intuitive current is impaired by morbid anxieties, human beings fight for their existence, believing that the circumstances and events unfolding on the screen of their lives are the result of pure chance!

> While the repetition of a given sound architecture can provide well-being, fortune and health, the ultimate goal of mantra practice is to help us rediscover our spiritual identity.

The human race halts its evolution by remaining shallow and fearful even though every individual is heir to the spirit's limitless opulence and supernatural powers. Fortunately, a great many doctors are beginning to emerge from the impasse into which scholastic teachings have plunged them. On this topic, the late Norman Cousins, author of *Anatomy of an Illness* and a former professor at the University of Los Angeles Faculty of Medicine, stated: "If I could give something to people, it would be to free them from their fears... because fear creates illness."

Fear results in cellular disorders and listening to harsh, distressing sounds generates an autosuggestion of fear. Consequently, it comes as no surprise that profoundly listening to spiritual resonances releases the subtle energies of the soul and gradually destroys all that casts a shadow on the human being's heart.

These mantric sound waves are a potent weapon in the already impressive arsenal of new vibratory medicine, which is, it should be noted, as ancient as Ayurvedic medicine—somewhere between three to five thousand years old. Dr. Richard Gerber, author of *Vibrational Medicine,* provides a glimpse of a multidimensional human being with limitless healing potential, which is beginning to be recognized even by conventional science:

> We tend to think that the human body is powered by electrophysiological forces (nerves, etc.), but this system is controlled by one of superior energies regulating cellular and biochemical processes. And this system of subtle energy is much closer in frequency to the life force. Some forms of vibratory medicine are carried out at levels of what we refer to as elevated spiritual realities and which are not widely accepted by conventional science. Certain factions within the conventional scientific community believe this, but scientific institutions

continue to reject these things, considering them to be eccentric…. Medicine as a whole is changing because there are well-trained doctors who are gradually becoming interested in complementary approaches and who see these studies as more credible. These approaches are not intended to replace current scientific theory, but to extend it.[50]

Whether it is crystals, sound vibrations, acupuncture, the astral body, floral essences or even surgery, we must come to understand that all these approaches are complementary; they are not opposed to one another. Healing amounts to freeing the body and mind from the negative energies that diminish them. The energy of mantras, phonic formulas whose vibratory effects exert a profound influence on our three main bodies (physical, mental and spiritual), can be successfully used in vibratory medicine and can immunize us against the anxieties at the root of most cellular imbalances.

As Gerber states, "Healing is allowing the reestablishment of an overall creative movement: that of the body and the soul, that of the individual and the planet."[51]

To listen to and sing spiritual sound vibrations while treading in the masters' footsteps constitutes the path to perfection and freedom from doubt and fear for all. This path is not only offered to students wishing to perfect their ideological research, but also to those who have already triumphed in their efforts, whether they are only interested in the fruits of their actions (*karma yogis*), impersonal philosophers (*jnani yogis*) or lovers of the Absolute (*bhakti yogis*).

The path of listening and song is not affected by

age, race, sex or social status. It is free, easy and without any strict rules concerning place or time. The pleasure of singing and listening to the sound of mantras awakens progressively within us. This method is not reserved for those who wish to succeed in self-realization practices; it is equally recommended for anyone who is attached to material life. All the masters of Vedas agree that this is a sure path to spiritual success.

THE enigma OF LIVING Repetition

Individuals who have failed to properly assimilate the strength released by the phenomenon of repetition sometimes criticize the practice of mantras. It should be recognized that this criticism is based on insufficient knowledge of the science of mantra and on incomplete experimentation with active musical repetition. On this subject, musicologist George Balan says:

> The message of sound is an enigma to our mind. He who feels that this enigma hides the key to spiritual liberation will obviously strive to solve it. The only way to do so is to repeat the mel-

ody until a symbiosis is achieved. This is a living repetition, and has nothing of the mechanic in it. Success is achieved only by letting the music reverberate within one's self as consciously as possible. The more the melody is interiorized, in other words, sung not so much with the lips as with the inner voice, the more it will permeate our depths, making them radiate. When practiced diligently, slowly but surely, this repetition will bring with it the solution to the enigma, a solution of a nature totally different from the solution arrived at through reasoning and sensed as a considerable increase in our psychic strength. This intimate work is nothing more than the musical expression of the laws underlying all authentic meditation, namely the confrontation of the enigma, which in the Zen tradition is called "koan" and the "digesting" of the meditation formula, better known under the Sanskrit word mantram, whose action on the soul can make of man a new Oedipus, conqueror of the inner Sphinx, source of agonizing enigmas.[52]

Thus, the repetition of a given sound formula is not an obstacle, rather, it is of valuable assistance, provided of course that it is not repeated mechanically or automatically. It is essential that the heart be entirely available and actively engaged in the repetition of the chant. If only the lips are involved and if the mind wanders, the heart will remain empty and the individual will find within neither the strength nor the desire to taste the mantra. This tasting—which has nothing at all in com-

mon with the pleasures of the senses or of the flesh, being far superior in intensity and quality—is the direct result of conscious repetition.

The individual who sets out sincerely on the royal path of repetition of the mantras can expect to experience sooner or later a joy that goes beyond and transcends all joys. The person's entire life may consequently be transformed. This experience does not belong exclusively to the Sanskrit culture.

In the *Philocaly* of the Russian Orthodox tradition, which the early Christian father Nicodemus described as the safeguard of intelligence and the infallible guide to contemplation, several allusions are found to this inexpressible superior pleasure that is born of prayer from the heart. In it, Isaac de Ninive, an extraordinary monk of the ninth century, writes of the mystical pleasure that springs from the repetition of his own mantra prayer, "Lord Jesus Christ, have pity on me, Son of God":

> He who succeeds in continuous prayer attains all virtues and at the same time, finds a spiritual dwelling. Whether he is asleep or awake, prayer never leaves his soul. While he eats, drinks, lies down, works, sleeps, the perfume of prayer is spontaneously exhaled from his soul. One should not confuse the joy of prayer with the vision of prayer:

the latter is stronger than the former. It sometimes happens that the chant of words is particularly smooth on the lips and that the same word is repeated endlessly without creating a feeling of satisfaction required to go beyond and onto the next word. Sometimes, the repetition of sacred words leads to a degree of contemplation and the prayer dies on the lips. He who experiences such contemplation enters into the realm of ecstasy. This is what we refer to as the vision within prayer; it is not an image or a shape invented by the imagination, as inexperienced fools claim.[53]

This state of ecstasy, this superior pleasure, is the ripened fruit of the music of the soul. When the therapeutic effects of sound combine with the effects of words, we witness the emergence of a supra-natural feeling. This feeling, which transcends mere sentimentality, is of a spiritual nature and can enlighten the entire being because it makes possible harmonic fusion with the source of all light. At this moment, the distinct soul can perceive the inconceivable music of forgotten worlds, remembering the pure love relationship that unites it with the great heavenly families. Unified, it recovers its immense powers and sings in unison with the whole of creation. This is what prompted Father Mersenne to write in his *Universal Harmony*, published in 1636, "The spirit begins to enjoy the music of the blessed when it hears the unison that causes it to recall its origin and the bliss it hopes for and awaits."

SOUND PENETRATES
THE OMNIPRESENT ETHER

The word is a gift from He through whom all lives, the *sat* (absolute existence) of which we are the infinitesimal living particles. This divine quality, this incomparable gift, is the origin of all human creation. Give a name to a being or an object and the being will exist, the object will manifest itself on the subtle plains of ether. Sound is not spread at the level of air, but of ether. This is why the sound, the word, the name, born of the mother word, penetrates all things, ether being the omnipresent subtle element on the physical plane. Consequently, as noted previously, if we continue to name an object, a particular quality or a being, the latter will manifest itself in matter. This creative process is, in fact, a question of continuity.

In the Buddhist *Vajrayana* doctrine, the *bija mantra "ah"*–corresponding to the letter A, the first in our alphabet–represents the mystery of the spoken word (*vak*). This mystery goes beyond that of the ordinary word. It is the audible symbol through which humans express themselves and it holds the power to transmit the work of truth. It is creative sound, the initiatory language that rekindles the spark of true spiritual light at the bottom of the heart of the radiant being, the happy and essentially immortal entity.

The letter A, word of mystery, holds the secret of

the creative sound energy of images, dreams, visions, thoughts—indeed, of all that is related to art, culture and science. This mystery of the word is more than divine; it is the universal intelligence itself. The Vedic scriptures corroborate this assertion.

In the tenth chapter of Bhagavad Gita Krishna tells Arjuna, "Among all letters, I am the A." *Akara,* the first letter of the Sanskrit alphabet, constitutes the beginning of all Vedic literature. No word can be pronounced without it. The letter A represents the origin of all sound. And the sound, or the word, is God Himself. As Krishna says in the seventh chapter of the same text, "I am the infinite that sustains all. I am the sound within ether."[54]

> If we continue to name an object, a particular quality or a being, the latter will manifest itself in matter. This creative process is, in fact, a question of continuity.

It is possible to perceive the divine presence through its countless sound energies, and thus, to realize its impersonal aspect. The impersonalist, for instance, will be content to perceive the Absolute in the sound born by ether throughout the universe. The personalist, on the other hand, will glorify the Absolute for allowing human beings to express their feelings, emotions, thoughts, joys and sorrows through the extraordinary means of the spoken word, music and song. This is recognition of the Absolute in all its aspects: impersonal, personal and localized. As Krishna states in the Gita: "I am the sacred syllable *om* in all of the Vedas.*"*

The *om,* also referred to as *omkara* and *pranava,* or the spiritual sound vibration that begins most Vedic incantations, emanates from the supreme being. Impersonalists prefer to hear the vibration of the sound of the *om-kara,* conceiving of the Absolute not as a divine person, but as divine light and peace. In fact, personalism and impersonalism are not in opposition. These two aspects of truth are perfectly complementary. For those who know the *causa causarum* and all that it is, has been and will be, all things involve at one and the same time the personal and the impersonal. Moreover, this is further detailed in Chaitanya's sublime doctrine, *achintya bhedabheda tattva,* or simultaneous unity and multiplicity.

a.u.m.: THE KEY TO TRANSFORMATION

The manner in which sound can give us the opportunity to contact transcendental realities is clearly established by Swami Bhaktivedanta in his commentary on the *Vedanta Sutra.* The impressive work of esoteric and devotional literature reads as follows:

> *abhvasen manasa suddham*
> *trivrd-brahmaksaram param*
> *mano yacchej jita-svaso*
> *brahma-bijam avismaran*

> After sitting down in a remote and pure place, the seeker must bring his thoughts back to the three absolute letters (A.U.M.) and, by regulating his breathing, must master his mental processes in order not to forget this spiritual key.[55]

Om, the *pranava,* the *omkara,* the sacred syllable formed by three absolute letters—A.U.M.—is the key, the seed of intimate self-realization. Reciting it mentally while regulating one's breathing—a spiritual technique created and practiced by great yogis and through which one achieves a state of profound oxygenation—makes it possible to master mental processes dominated by the ways of matter. Swami A. C. Bhaktivedanta explains that, in this way, it is entirely possible to cure oneself of harmful mental habits.

Certain schools of meditation teach that it is necessary to "kill" the mind. This is a serious mistake. Indeed, regardless of the method used in doing so, nothing is more harmful than attempting to suppress mental activity and desire. Yet more often than not, this is what is attempted in misguided yoga centers *(ashrams).*

It is important to realize that mental activity and desire cannot be halted. It is, however, possible to cultivate the desire to act in light of the goal of ultimate evolution. It is vain to try to "kill" the mind. Rather, it is the very nature of the object of the thought itself that should be transformed.

Bhaktivedanta Swami points out: "Since the mental represents the pivot, the axis which directs the active organs, if we transform the nature of mental functions—thinking, feeling and wanting—the activity of the senses will be modified accordingly. Only the spiritual sound is capable of bringing forth the desired mental and sensory transformation and the omkara (A.U.M.) forms the first seed, the key to all spiritual sound vibration. The power of spiritual sound is such that it can even heal those who suffer mental imbalance."[56]

The words of the mystic poet Krishnadas Kaviraj in *Sri Chaitanya Charitamrita,* are clear on the subject of this extraordinary vibration: *prandva' se mahavakva/vedera nidana isvara/svarupa pranava sarva' va-dhama.* This verse, found in seventh chapter of the *Adi-lila* section, says: "The Vedic sound vibration *om (omkara),* the most important word in all of Vedic literature, is the basis of all vibrations. Therefore, it should be accepted as the sound representation of the God's sublime personality and should be perceived as the trustee of all cosmic manifestations." However, Krishna himself does not hesitate to declare in the Gita:

om itv ekaksaram brahma
vyaharam mam anusmaran
yah prayati tyajan deham
sa yati paramain gatim

This verse indicates that *om* is the direct representation of God.[57] If, at the moment of physical death, we can simply remember this unique mantra, we leave our body with the memory of the divine presence and consequently, we are immediately transferred to spiritual planes.

The sincere student who understands that the *omkara* is the sound representation of the Divine will realize that the power of *om,* sung in light of this awareness, is in all aspects identical to the power of the Holy Names (Buddha, Yahwe, Jehovah, Allah, Krishna, Cristos, Adonais...).

In his thesis, the *Bhagavat-sandarbha,* the devotional philosopher Jiva Goswami asserts that *om* is considered to be the sound vibration of the divine name. Only this vibration can deliver the soul from the claws of illusion *(maya)*. The great commentator Sridhara Swami describes the *omkara* as the seed of deliverance from the physical worlds.

The great reformer Chaitanya, known as the avatar of divine love, stipulates in his teachings that *omkara* holds all the powers of the Absolute and is in no way different from God. To sing it amounts to directly encountering the personality of the creative forces of the universe in its sound form.

The *Mandukya Upanishad* declares that what is possible to perceive on spiritual planes is nothing short of an extension of the absolute power of *om.* Further, the Goswamis, the direct disciples of Chaitanya, provide a detailed explanation of *om* by analyzing it according to the terms of its alphabetical constituents:

> *akarenocyate krsnah*
> *sarva-lokaika-nayakah*
> *ukarenoeyate radha*
> *makaro jiva-vacakah*

Omkara is a combination of the letters A, U and M. The letter A refers to the friend of  all living entities and the ruler of all material and spiritual planets. According to the science of mantras, it is the static wave. The letter U indicates the power of divine pleasure *(Srimati Radharani)*, or the wave of resonance. The letter M indicates the living beings. It is the oscillating wave, a marginal energy.

Impersonalist philosophers *(mayavadis)* consider

several Vedic mantras as the *mahamantra,* or great mantra. According to the Bhagavad Gita, most of these mantras are in fact only accessories. The *omkara* can be considered, however, a *mahavakya* or *mahamantra,* which is nondifferent from God. Such a realization cannot be proven in a laboratory setting and is possible only by simply chanting the sacred name of the divine presence, *omkara.*

> The conditioned being's spiritual advancement toward the Absolute is related to the purification of the senses.

This combination of sound vibrations (A.U.M.) has not been invented or fabricated by a human being. In reality, this transcendental sound possesses a spiritual and absolute power. By singing and listening to its particular harmonics, we realize that this power is divine and unifying energy in all its aspects.

The *omkara* is identical to what we sense is God. This presence cannot be seen or heard by imperfect senses. Therefore, the conditioned being's spiritual advancement toward the Absolute is related to the purification of the senses.

Training based on a technique of respiratory mastery combined with a silent, inner recitation of the *omkara* is essential for anyone who wishes to see spiritual realizations appear in the mind, where all sensory activities reside.

Chanting and listening to the *omkara* are the first steps toward spiritual enlightenment. In general, we suffer from an incomplete perception of the universe. We are incapable of realizing the forms or sublime and personal names of the Absolute because matter impairs our senses. As long as this state persists, it is impossible for us to concentrate our thoughts directly on the personal aspect of truth. By following the impersonal discipline that consists of listening and chanting the *omkara*, the mind gradually frees itself from all preconceived ideas that weigh it down and one is able to contemplate the personal features of the all-powerful and all-loving hidden presence.

Progressively, spiritual sound succeeds in dislodging the mind from sensory activities. This sound vibration sustains the power of intelligence, which is then able to control the senses. Hence, the mind gradually loses the habit of being absorbed in solely material action. It does not sink into sterile inactivity, however, because it eventually succeeds in embracing the service of love offered to the Divine, and in fully establishing itself in a perfect state of consciousness.

THE MYSTERIES OF HARMONIC FREQUENCIES

While many skeptics believe that the sound wave acts on a psycho-physiological level, along with all derivatives of attention that is not the case. Researcher Alec Washco found that the more melodic and rhythmic elements are defined in a harmonic combination, the more precise the physiological reactions they trigger will be and the more we can be assured of their manifestation in the body and mind of the listener. It should be noted, however, that the same musical energies produce different physiological reactions among people, depending upon the individual's emotional state.

What is the mechanism at the origin of these reactions in body and mind? Researcher La Monte Young puts forward a hypothesis that is as interesting from the perspective of music in general as it is regarding the sound vibrations involved in the incantations of ancient traditions. His hypothesis provides a rational explanation for the mysterious effect of sung mantras or of prayers used throughout time, in all parts of the planet, by people conscious of the power of sound. According to Young: "When a specific series of harmonically related frequencies is continuous, in a more definite way it produces or stimulates a psychological state which is felt by the listener given the fact that such a series of frequencies will continually trigger a specific series of auditory nerves which, in turn, will carry out the same transmission operation from a periodic model of impulses to the series of points determined by their counterparts in the cerebral cortex."[58]

This idea brings to mind the famous Hindu *raga,* the exact scales of which are said to always provoke the same effects. Edith Lecours, who studied La Monte Young's hypothesis in the course of her in-depth research on the actuality and development of *musicotherapy,* believes that this idea could also be applied to other music often considered "primitive," where the therapeutic function finds its precision and its circumspection in the use of sounds, insofar as these sounds are properly prolonged and insofar as they permeate the individual, as is the case, for example, with Tibetan chants.

om mani padme hūm: the healing compassion

It is commonly accepted that among other effects, the syllables *om mani padme hūm* produce compassion. While there is a measure of the multidimensional in mantric formulas, it seems that it is mainly the energies of compassion that result from the listening to, or the chanting of, this combination of seed-syllables and word-symbols.

This mantra has often been translated as, "Oh thee, jewel in the lotus," but in my opinion, mantras should not be adapted to current language through philosophical interpretations. They are what they are, and the energy that emanates from them should above all be felt physically, psychically or spiritually, rather than being intellectually analyzed through reasoning.

To illustrate this particular point, consider the bumblebee. According to mathematical theory, the bumblebee should not be able to fly because its body is not proportionate to its wingspan. But the bumblebee eschews mathematics and flies freely. It relies on its instinct, not on reason.

Mantras resemble the bumblebee: they are not reasonable. They put aside the intellect and function simply by liberating the energies that correspond to the resonances they carry. Hence, if we wish to understand the sound formulas, we have no physical means other than basic experience and the experience of the multiple associations of the mysterious forces contained in their word-symbols. The energy of mantras simply cannot be understood in any other way. Rather than wondering how it is mathematically possible to fly, would we not be better off saving precious time, opening the doors of our minds and flying on the wings of sound, propelled by the reactors of mantric light toward the invisible dimensions of existence?

This being said, it is likely that in light of the data compiled by La Monte Young, in the near future some laboratory research will be undertaken and researchers will discover that a given mantra can indeed produce a specific psychological state, with this state being triggered by the stimulation of a particular series of auditory neurons, as Young described. We will then better understand how a given sound can result in a given psychological or physical state.

Nevertheless, we know that the mantra *om mani padme hūṁ* leads to a feeling of compassion, automatically followed by general well-being characterized by a relaxed body and a mind at peace.

In his book *Mantras or the Power of Sacred Words,* John Blofeld writes:

> For the non-initiate, Mani is often used as a spell to ward off all types of misfortune.... Recently, Professor Charles Luk (in Chinese, Lu K'uan-Yu), a remarkable researcher and writer and an authority on Chinese Buddhism, wrote to me to draw my attention to the therapeutic qualities of the mantra in cases of psychic illnesses such as hallucinations and other similar disorders. The patient

must practice daily. I myself was healed within one evening from an illness I had contracted on one of my trips in the mountains of North China. Having fallen from my mule because I suddenly began to feel faint, people from the nearest inn had come to my rescue. There, I sank into a deep comatose state. When I regained consciousness, a Mongol lama standing at the foot of my bed was reciting in a low voice the *om mani padme hūm*. The result was wonderful! Pain and fatigue disappeared and the following morning, I was as bright and lively as I had been on the very first day of my journey. Of course, in such circumstances, it is easy to argue that the mantra's beneficial effect is solely psychological, a point I do not contest; but things are not as simple as they may appear to be....The mantra—psychically related to an identical element in the psyche of those it is used for—draws enormous strength from the power accumulated over the course of centuries by sacred groups involving numberless practitioners.[59]

a PURIFYING PROCeSS

The service of love offered to the Divine manifests by listening, chanting and remembering what is related to it in any of its multiple personal representations. It is established in the perfect ecstasy, or *samadhi,* representing the highest degree of the previously prescribed method.

Even in a meditative state in which mental activity is temporarily subdued, the mind recalls past actions that spring from the subconscious, creating an obstacle for the soul wishing to dedicate itself to spiritual realization. This explains the importance of the direct method of listening and chanting the mantras of the Holy Names.

> यामिमां पुष्पितां वाचं प्रवदन्त्यविपश्चितः ।
> वेदवादरताः पार्थ नान्यदस्तीति वादिनः ॥४२॥
> कामात्मानः स्वर्गपरा जन्मकर्मफलप्रदाम् ।
> क्रियाविशेषबहुलां भोगैश्वर्यगतिं प्रति ॥४३॥

In many instances, the Vedic scriptures stipulate the superiority of this method. They designate it as *yoginam,* the surest path to spiritual emancipation. Even human beings experiencing mental turmoil are ensured of progress if they take this path under the direction of a qualified teacher *(guru).* Thus the impersonal spiritual sound vibration (the *omkara),* the quintessence of all mantras, leads us to the shores of the sacred names.

Chanting these mantras, more specifically the *om,* holds the power to cleanse the mind. This purification process eliminates all karmic dust accumulated from time immemorial. The results of the chant can be perceived directly, without an intermediary. Whoever chants or listens to any of these numerous words of power, even if only for a short time each day, is purified from material contamination sooner or later and feels transcendental pleasure. There is no medicine more powerful than the Holy Names. The active influence of their sound sequences, which can be emitted through the intermediary of human language, is the perfect tool for awakening the soul.

MUSIC: THE PHYSICS OF THE SOUL

In his revolutionary book *Quantum Healing: Exploring the Frontiers of Mind-Body Medicine* (a work I recommend to all those interested in learning more about the therapeutic power of sacred sound), Dr. Deepak Chopra writes, "Finer subatomic particles would seem to be waves of form, vibrations called 'superstrings,' or supra-sensitive chords, because they react in exactly the same way as the strings of a violin...."[60] These "superstrings" develop everywhere in the universe and their number is infinite. They underlie all creation. Since this subatomic network is located beyond the limited reality of our three dimensions, no current laboratory instrument, regardless of its power, can observe it.

This very recent theory of physics is surprisingly close to the Vedic explanation that all cosmic transformation is supported by a creative power, much as the pearls of a necklace are threaded on a string.

Thus, nothing is inert or isolated. Everything vibrates interactively. Each organ is sustained by a particular "superstring," which must be well tuned if the organ is to play in key. Therefore, we can no longer consider the body to be a mass of inert flesh. The Ayurvedic vision shows us that it is a network of *sutras,* or conductive wires. The body is a sound box.

The best way to act upon a vibratory frequency is to emit a corresponding vibratory frequency using the well-known phenomenon of resonance. This explains, for instance, the success obtained by Dr. Desikachar who directs an institute in Madras, India, where Ayurvedic medicine, yoga and song are taught. The National Department of Health of the Indian government has recognized the institute as serving the public good. Cécile Beaudet and Richard Belfer brilliantly describe the institute's use of song in an article entitled "Healing Music."

> The energy of mantras, phonic formulas whose vibratory effects exert a profound influence on our three main bodies (physical, mental and spiritual), can be successfully used in vibratory medicine and can immunize us against the anxieties at the root of most cellular imbalances.

The article quotes Dr. Desikachar as saying: "Our ancestors had classified the letters of the alphabet in different categories. Certain sounds, HA with an aspirated H, for example, have a stimulating effect. Others, like MA, sung softly in a low-pitched note, have a calming effect."[61]

Beaudet and Belfer report that this knowledge has led the institute's teachers to use song with pregnant women as a preparation for delivery, with asthmatics to help them exhale, with people suffering from hypertension to help them relax and with individuals who suffer from backaches to correct both their breathing and their posture.

In the article, the authors also quote Jill Purce, therapist and voice coach who, in the course of her work with German composer and theorist Karlheinz Stockhausen and the Tibetan Buddhist masters, discovered that:

A great many of our contemporaries are dissatisfied with their life and feel that another part of themselves could be developed. In such a case, healing—for patients—does not necessarily involve working directly on the symptom. I consider illness to be the expression of a more deeply rooted imbalance that must be corrected. For each of us, each moment can bring with it the pretext to regret the past or to fear the future. Because of this anxiety, things are less and less similar to what we expect. Depending on our weak points, this disequilibrium will manifest itself in the form of a cold, a backache or a cancer.[62]

This disequilibrium is also a series of false notes, a cacophony, mental at first, then cellular. Calming our mental agitation, therefore, will have a beneficial effect on us. For this purpose, mantric energies are genuinely useful, perhaps even irreplaceable. This is the reason why a Tibetan master might suggest meditative exercises that will lead us to visualize a letter, or a series of letters, a *mantra,* and then to sing it. By chanting or listening to the mantra we feel a vibratory effect that calms mental activity, which is often overwhelming and uncontrollable, in order that the mantra may act directly on specific parts of the body.

As Dr. Richard Gerber stated so accurately: "We already use vibratory medicine without realizing it: all these forms of treatment are based on energy. The medical establishment is not aware of the fact that it already calls upon energy in the course of the healing process. Ultrasound is already used to dissolve kidney stones:

this is sound energy, vibratory medicine."[63]

Sound, like electricity and light, is a conventional form of electromagnetic energy. If used in harmony with the subtle energy of consciousness (activated with effective mental visualization combined with the power of creative assertion), in a sense, this form of energy becomes all-powerful, because it is transmitted to the deepest oscillations of the organism through the vector of the "superstrings." Sound is the surgeon's new scalpel, but this is a scalpel that knows nothing of pain, that involves none of the dangers of general anesthetics. Moreover, it is more pleasant to submit oneself ("to put oneself under") musical energies than to yield one's body, often in blind faith, to the hands of those who still practice medicine with the heavy artillery of modern surgery.

Thus, vibratory energy partly accounts for the results obtained by using the therapeutic power of music and mantras. This subatomic sound current being retroactive, the superstring network also explains why the Bhagavad Gita defines the source principle as "the sound that traverses ether." This is the omnipresence that sustains all. At this level, there are no religious concepts (in the Catholic or Hindu sense of the word); there is an intuitive vision, knowledge, application of what has

been "seen" by a long-standing tradition as well as by scientific experimentation (quantum physics, microvibratory physics, vibratory medicine and so forth).

The physicist Fritjof Capra has appropriately compared this physical omnipresence of vibrating subatomic particles to the dance of the god Shiva. These particles enlighten us as to how the primitive, or original, human, while imitating the natural sounds of his environment, vested himself with the power of the life forces at the source of these sounds. Science has not yet "discovered" the subtle effect of retroactive waves. Hence, the original human was not as low on the evolutionary scale as we have been led to believe.

Conscious electromagnetic sound energy forms the foundation of the ritual songs and dances of many cultures' shamans or medicine men. This same energy was used during the Brahman ceremonies of the Vedic culture and in Egyptian initiations during which powerful sound and mantric structures were sung and heard.

Today, particle accelerators have led to the discovery of a supersensitive network, or current. We have a better understanding of how mantras can trigger vibratory effects that have a far-reaching influence at the atomic and subatomic levels of the physical, the psychic and the spiritual. Egyptians called music the "physics of the soul." Far be it from Dr. Chopra, for whom DNA is the messenger of the quantum world, to contradict them. It was through this infinite network of superstrings that the Orpheus of mythology restored life to Eurydice, thanks to the harmonious sound of his harp and the gentle power of his voice. Dr. Frank Alper, founder of the Arizona Metaphysical Society in Phoenix, frequently lectures on metaphysics. His work elucidates the therapeutic use of sounds, colors and crystals (vibratory medicine) in ancient traditions. These sound rituals or mantras are the means through which a given vibratory force is transmitted to an organ, a muscle, a vertebra, a thought, through the subtle subatomic particle vector. By providing the whole body (physical, emotional, ethereal) with a perfect harmonic vibration, such as the primordial sound *om,* for example, it is possible to fine-tune the musical instrument that represents our organism as a whole.

In *From Sound Springs Light,* Hélène Caya writes: "The listening techniques of inner resonance and realignment remain first and foremost a means to prevent serious disturbances within the organism. Ideally, each day we would go about, checking on the small disorders which, like intruders, disturb our peace and equilibrium."[64]

> When the therapeutic effects of sound combine with the effects of words, we witness the emergence of a supra-natural feeling.

This is exactly what a person who hears or listens to a mantric meditative song, whether consciously or not, does. Whether it is a song from Egypt, India, America, Africa or from another planet, is only relatively important. Each day, at home, or on a regular basis at workshops, it is possible to reharmonize our minds and our bodies through sound. Consider it preventive and therapeutic action. This overall harmonization affects cardiac rhythm, blood circulation, breathing and digestion as well as directly affecting the glands—extraordinary body parts that play an important role in our psychic and spiritual equilibrium.

A little more than one hundred years ago, no one knew that the endocrine glands existed. However, the sages of

Vedic civilization were well aware of their existence some 5,000 years ago. Each gland, according to the Vedic scriptures, has a vibratory frequency that coincides with that of a bija mantra, that is to say, a seed sound or root sound. Each gland corresponds to a state of consciousness, which is itself localized in a "center," or *chakra*.

The next chapter proposes exercises in which the centers of consciousness (chakras) are retuned to the proper frequency. It is not necessary to understand intellectually the functioning of this kind of exercise, which puts into practice the fundamentals of vibratory medicine. Egyptians adopted the same practices in their monastery-clinic called the Temple of Beauty.

Whether or not we can logically analyze the precise nature of fire, it continues to burn. In the same way, sound exerts its effect. The state of fulfillment and health it provokes when methodically applied endures the test of any thorough scientific examination for the simple and obvious reason that it does indeed have an effect.

Figures illustrating the sound method known as psychophony (a method patented by the Paris Academy

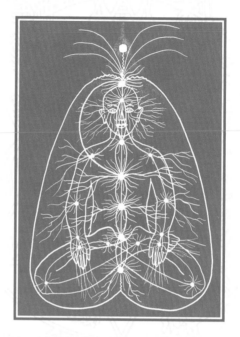

of Science), published in Marie-Louise Aucher's book *Sonorous Man,* show a marked similarity between the points in the body that vibrate in harmony with certain notes and the points used in acupuncture. When asked how a psychophonic sound test and acupuncture are related, Aucher replied: "The Chinese have named the outline of acupuncture points 'the Governing Vessel which is in command of psychological and physical life forces.' Resonance zones are related to points of assent (a 'point of assent' is 'a harmonic junction point'). Acupuncturists activating these points with their needles have recognized and used these harmonic relationships over the course of centuries."[65] In the exercises in the next chapter, it is through soft sound waves, instead of metal needles, that the chakras are made to vibrate.

For instrumentalists, and to give one last detail on the experimental use of musical notes related to mantras, it is preferable to respect the Pythagorean scale (A3 = 432 frequencies). In 1953, at an international conference held in London, it was arbitrarily decided that the official value of A should be raised, and set at 440 Hz. What prompted the decision to raise the official frequency of A, already too high at the time (at 435 Hz)? Apparently no one knows. What strange reasoning brought about this change in traditional musical harmony, which was founded on the rigorous observation of the rhythms of nature? The Egyptian lyre and the Celtic harp are tuned to an A comprising 432 frequencies (which corresponds, of course, to the Pythagorean scale).

Knowledge has been lost and must be rediscovered. Originally, long before Pythagoras's time, the scale was calculated in relation to the position of the seven planets in the solar system. All the music of the spheres is founded upon this precept. All the divine and sacred numbers of the initiatory traditions on Earth are founded on this real-  ity, which vibrates to the rhythm of the planets. Since 1953, man is no longer "in tune" with the laws of the Universe. A dangerous error threatens the equilibrium of both macrocosm and microcosm.

Since 1953, all musical frequencies broadcast twenty-four hours a day around the world are "out of tune" with cosmic vibratory rhythms. How is it then possible to be surprised by the fact that the Earth seems to be drying out and that the advent of the age of consciousness has been slowed down?

One of the gravest responsibilities of the new composers of this new age is to retune their instruments to the universal frequency. Obviously, all cosmic rhythms and numbers are intimately linked to one another. The total of the figures in each is always nine (3 x 3) or a multiple of nine: 54 (half of the Vedic and Tibetan 108); 72 (the Pythagorean sacred number); 234 (the symmetrical axial number of 432); 432 (the sacred number of the Druids or bardec A); 504 (sacred number of southern Asia, 432 + 72); and 666 (sacred number of the Book of Revelation). Bodily frequencies vibrate in harmony with cosmic frequencies. The physical body vibrates *with* the galactic body.

The heart beats at a rate of 72 times per minute. The sun takes 72 years (7 + 2 = 9) to travel through one degree in the zodiac. The moon's vibratory frequency is 216 (72 x 3). Everything is linked, always.

Can we reasonably think, or hope, that an energetic musical vibration that is out of tune with the cosmos could have, on a long-term basis, a reharmonizing and beneficial effect? Music that does not hold sacred the laws of life cannot be as effective as a harmonic sound wave faithful to the dance of the universe.

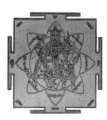

4

mantra yoga and the healing names of god

contemplative sound

 As noted in the previous chapter, mantra practice, or contemplative sound, is found in all cultures and religious systems and is not exclusive to Eastern traditions. Advanced souls who have followed the path of authentic Christianity, regardless of denominational persuasion, have reached the highest summits of purity and of indestructible inner joy through the famous "prayer of the heart" or other effective incantations. In the revealed writings of this same tradition, saints have found the path to salvation through contemplative sound.

On this topic, *Accounts of a Russian Pilgrim* (author unknown) quotes Pierre Damascene's text, which is part of the illustrious *Philocaly*:

> It is good to train oneself to invoke the Name of the Lord, more than to train the breathing, at all times, in all places, on all occasions. The adept says:

"Pray incessantly." In this, he teaches that it is necessary to remember the Inner God at all times, in all places and in all things. If you make something, you should think of the maker of all things that exist. If you see the light, remember He who has given it to you. If you consider the sky, the Earth, the sea and all things they contain, admire and glorify He who has created them. If you cover yourself with a garment, think of He who has given it to you and thank the Provider of your existence. In brief, may all gestures be a cause to celebrate the Creator; thus, you will pray incessantly and your soul will always be happy.[66]

This process is so simple and accessible because we all possess human emotion. The thought expressed in the Bhagavad Gita is in absolute agreement with that of the *Philocaly*:

> *yat karosi yad asnasi*
> *yaj juhosi dadasi yat*
> *yat tapasyasi kaunteya*
> *tat kurusva mad arpanam*

Whatever you do, eat, sacrifice and give, whatever austerity you practice, let it be an offering to Me.[67]

The Sufi tradition also accords great importance to the contemplation of the divine principle by listening to mystical sounds. According to Sourate 17.44 of the Koran, every creature is in a constant state of prayer.

The commentator Purjavadi says that this song of praise consists of a harmony that the Absolute has placed within each entity. In a work entitled *Music and Ecstasy,* which explores the vast field of mystical and ecstatic music within the Muslim world, expert Jean During explains that according to tradition: "The silent song of creatures can be perceived by sages of enlightened heart, as was the harmony of the spheres. Abdulkarim Jili refers to a degree of enlightenment where the divine is revealed through the being's attributes as a listener. To some, God reveals Himself through the quality of hearing."[68]

The Sufi practices the *dhirkr,* a technique of verbal memorizing, and a kind of repetitive litany able to provide the *dhawq,* or taste, a direct experience. It is this taste, this feeling, this immense pleasure that is the answer of the Absolute, a mystical pleasure offered in response to the contemplative sound. For initiates of mystical sound, the ecstatic feeling that captivates them during musical hearing *(sama)* comes from luminous visions that appear and disappear. These visions are also fleeting intuitive states, but nevertheless they are unforgettable.

When these magnificent flashes of lightning cross the sky of their consciousness, initiates are moved by such happiness that for them, all worries related to the the bodies are annihilated. They know they will never forget those confidential moments during which the identity of their inner being was revealed. Faithfully following the instructions of their guide, they absorb their thought in the inner esoteric incantation. The power of the prayer-song is such that it suddenly reveals a state, a universal knowledge that was buried in the singer's farthest depths.

By constant prayer to the Absolute, the practitioner and the listener alike experience subtle states that originate in the unseen world. These states do not come from without because the realm of light is everywhere within. The sacred song, audible only to the liberated and serene ear, brings nothing to the heart that it does not already have; it suddenly brings to the surface what was already there for all eternity.

THE SHABDA, A CONSCIOUS ENERGY OF LIGHT

There are two precise functions of listening to mantra. On one hand, it provokes a certain relaxation and can even go further by stimulating the elimination of toxic substances, thus healing the body and mind. On the other hand, and this is undoubtedly its most important role, it leads us toward a true appreciation of our intimate being and toward awareness of the *atma,* the soul within us.

Music relating to the words of power is a manifestation of the *shabda,* or primordial sound. It is an energy endowed with creative and transformative powers. This energy comes from God and is God. The *shabda* does not function through the intermediary of physical sound vibrations. It is energy of conscious light. We should not attribute too much importance to the manner in which mantras are pronounced, however. The sound components that make up their structure are of little importance in themselves. This explains why variations of the syllable *om (ung* in Tibetan, *ang* in Chinese and *ong* in Japanese; and even the *amen* of the Judeo-Christian tradition) produce the same mantric effect!

The *shabda* is the inner sound, the nonmaterial vibration endowed with the power of liberating the sleeping forces ensconced within us since the dawn of time. We are all the heirs and holders of these subtle energies. Born of the universal consciousness, each being represents an individual divine particle, a "son of God." Regardless of where the individual soul resides in its evolution, it has the power and the right to awaken its psychic and spiritual abilities. The sound vibration that induces this is not necessarily perceived by our senses. Awakened by the *shabda*—the original inner sound—our subtle energies disentangle the centers of our ethereal bodies and untie the chakras rendered sterile and inert by living in disagreement with the rhythm of life. Thus, the spiritual sound vibration—the mantra—makes the inner *shabda* vibrate in sympathy. And the *shabda* is the only force capable of healing illusion *(maya)* and capable of transmuting the coal of matter into diamonds of the spirit.

David Bohn, a student of Einstein, arrived at a similar conclusion. In some of his most important articles, he described a holographic universe, calling for a new order in physics. In his opinion, what appears to be a stable, tangible, visible and audible world is an illusion. If matter is dynamic, ephemeral, kaleidoscopic, in perpetual movement, it cannot be real.

In fact, according to the Vedas the world is real,

yet transitory. Beyond this world of passage exists an underlying order, a matrix of a superior reality. The Vedic scriptures confirm the ephemeral nature of matter, just as advanced physics has discovered more recently. According to the Bhagavad Gita, "Incessantly, day after day, the day breaks, and each time myriads of entities are brought back to existence. Incessantly, night after night, the night falls and with it comes their annihilation, about which they can do nothing. However, another world exists, eternal, beyond the two states of matter, manifested and non-manifested. The supreme world, which never perishes; when everything in the universe is dissolved, it remains intact."[69]

The *shabda*'s nonmaterial sound, which denotes the absolute consciousness, holds the power to bring the conditioned being into the very midst of the invisible reality that exists permanently beyond the physical, mental and intellectual sensory perceptions.

The sound holds the key to the mysteries of life and creation and the maintenance of the universe. Sound vibration is also perceived as the best way to free oneself from material conditioning and slavery. Throughout the ages, philosophers have posited that the living entity is in a state resembling sleep. The best way to awaken someone is to call his name until he arises from his sleep. In this context, the analogy of the sleeper awakened by the sound of his name is an accurate one, because the individual who is bewitched and poisoned by the soporific impermanent can be awakened to the

> Music relating to the words of power is a manifestation of the *shabda,* or primordial sound. It is an energy endowed with creative and transformative powers. This energy comes from God and is God.

eternal reality of transcendental resonances.

Transcendental resonances can be heard by listening to and chanting the sacred injunctions *(shabda-brahma)* or any other revealed scriptures, such as the *Chilarn-Balam,* the "Book of Books," the sacred jewel of pre-Colombian peoples. These activities are able to make the living beings' inner *shabda* vibrate and free them from the blockages restricting them to the confines of the physical world. As the *Srimad Bhagavatam* states, "The Absolute is in the heart of each being in the form of the supersoul; He purifies the heart that develops the steadfast desire to hear His message from all physical desire."

The transcendental sound, the message of the essential being contained in the *shabda-brahma* is in no way different from universal truth. Thus, each time one listens or conveys this sound vibration, the soul of the inner God manifests its personal presence under the form of a sound holding all its power. This power alone is able to purify the intimate being from all its impediments. The state of well-being that inevitably follows represents a unique experience, unforgettable and profoundly initiatory.

This purifying *shabda-brahma* is found in all great revelations aimed at awakening and elevating the human soul. Whether these beneficial revelations originate from Eastern or Western civilizations is genuinely unimportant. What matters is the knowledge they carry—universal, practical and useful knowledge concerning the complete, uncompromising healing of environmental and psychological wounds caused by the planetary mistakes of those who pursue material exploitation at all costs.

It is necessary and urgent that the unique experience of spiritual sound vibration be experienced everywhere in the world; this experience triggers a profound change in the hearts of individuals. Through this process, human beings gradually develop their potential consciousness and renew contact with the supersoul within. They then regain the awareness of being linked in essence to everything that surrounds them, to oceans, forests, rivers, mountains and plains. They understand that harm inflicted upon any aspect of creation is actually damage done to them. From then on, they cease to bemoan their fate, putting an end to self-destruction.

REHARMONIZATION OF THE CENTERS OF CONSCIOUSNESS THROUGH SOUND AND COLOR

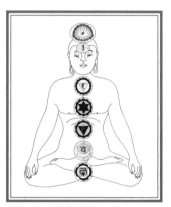

In general, modern medicine recognizes only one body: the physical body. However, for millennia, human beings who have succeeded in elevating themselves beyond physical sensations by accelerating their molecular vibrations have recognized, through experience, the existence of an immaterial body far more subtle than our obvious physical covering. As it does not consist of physical atoms, this subtle or *astral body* cannot be perceived by our five senses. For this reason, human beings who have not gone through the process of purification aimed at developing clairvoyance, clairaudience, telepathy, intuition or psychic powers in general are doomed to remain in the limited space of their physical senses.

Genuine security rests on one thing only: the harmonization of the subtle body. It is only when the body vibrates in sympathy with cosmic equilibrium that all physical life thrives. The appearance of the physical body is the direct reflection of the state of the subtle body. The anatomy of the subtle body has been known since time immemorial, and the Vedic scriptures explain it in detail.

Ancient Chinese literature has also contributed important information on the topic. Thus, we know that the astral body is covered with specific minute points, which the Chinese called *hsié*, corresponding to the points used in acupuncture. By activating them, it is possible to free crucial energy currents related to the proper functioning of our entire being. Certain points are particularly noteworthy, for instance, the centers of energy, called *chakras* in Sanskrit. The word chakra means wheel of energy-consciousness. *Nadis,* a system of subtle nerves, link these centers to one another. Clairvoyance shows these *chakras* under the form of spirals strangely resembling the black holes in space. The chakras are extremely powerful transmitters and receivers. All of the emotional functions of the individual are affected if the chakras are unbalanced or out of tune. The manner in which existence is perceived directly depends on whether or not the *chakras* are properly harmonized.

> The analogy of the sleeper awakened by the sound of his name is an accurate one, because the individual who is bewitched and poisoned by the soporific impermanent can be awakened to the eternal reality of transcendental resonances.

All sorts of tensions and fears usually block these centers. This accumulation of negative emotions prevents us from the full enjoyment of life's heritage, which is, according to divine law, an inexhaustible treasure of serenity and abundance at all levels.

As nothing in the galaxy is left to chance, it is possible to exercise an immediate action on the *chakras.* Each of them reverberates *with* a particular frequency and corresponds to specific planes of consciousness. When these points are aligned and vibrate in harmony, the feeling experienced goes beyond human language. The most accurate words to express this feeling of plenitude are strength, health, beauty, knowledge, success, living light and pure love. These centers of consciousness are seven in number and their counterparts in the various planes, visible and invisible, moveable and immovable, are unlimited.

1. THE consciousness-center of earth (*muladhara chakra*)

This is literally the support, the basis of the incarnated being.  Located at the perineum (between the anus and the genitals), it constitutes the floor of the individual. This center links us to Mother Earth and to all living entities inhabiting it. All our existential fears reside here. The planet that rules this chakra is Pluto and a beneficial stone to influence this chakra is the ruby.

The root center can easily be cleansed from these useless and dangerous tensions by the color red, the note C and the *bija mantra* Lam, by letting the mental processes become peacefully absorbed by the corresponding positive assertions:

> I feel perfectly linked to Earth and to all beings on it. I love them and they love me. I thus have nothing to fear from them or them from me. All is well.
> Through visualization, I let the color red, the note C, and the sound vibration *Lammmm...* dissolve my fears. If something particularly frightens me, I allow myself to think about it, to visualize it and to admit that it really frightens me. I then let the color red and the Lam sound transform this fear into cosmic dust. Tensions ease. I feel integrated into Earth and related to the beings upon it. Nothing exists in the universe that can frighten me. I feel perfectly protected and supported. The omnipresent forces of good love me and protect me. I am the immortal soul, unalterable and eternally happy.

2. THE CONSCIOUSNESS-CENTER OF WATER (SVADHISTHANA CHAKRA)

This is the miraculous tree, the totem, and the innermost seat of the being, our individualization, and our foundation. It is the chakra of sexuality, related to the water element. Creativity, freedom from sexual frustrations, blood circulation and social relations depend on its proper functioning. The planet that rules this chakra is Mars and a favorable stone for this chakra is coral.

This chakra reacts to the color orange, to the note D

and to the seed vibration Vam. The assertions that correspond to it are:

I visualize the color orange and I sing the mantra *Vammmm...* on the note D. I feel that the synthesis of these frequencies cleanses and reactivates my reproductive organs. This action perfectly balances the masculine and feminine energies within me. Consequently, I am able to give and to receive; I am able to create everything that I can possibly conceive of. If I know that I bear within me a given residue, a complex, a sexual frustration, a specific trauma, I allow myself to think about it, to visualize it and to accept that it really exists, without trying to ignore it or to hide it. I then let the color and the sound dissolve this tension and make it completely disappear.

I know that from now on, my sexual relations will be beautiful and free from fear, violence and egoism. I am able to create beautiful things. All my relationships are harmonious. I get along well with everyone. I have no more resentment toward anyone and no one is resentful toward me. I do not hold a grudge against anyone and no one does against me. The forces of good and love protect me, everywhere and always. I am the immortal soul, indestructible, perfectly conscious and eternally happy. I am a part of God. I am divine. I am at one with God in quality. I am of divine essence.

3. THE CONSCIOUSNESS-CENTER OF FIRE (*manipura chakra*)

 In Sanskrit, manipura means "jewel-filled stronghold." This center is located near the navel. It is genuinely filled with treasures since it is the seat of power, energy, personal feelings, purpose, free will and ambition. It is related to fire. It is the chakra of the solar plexus, at the pit of the stomach. The planet that rules this chakra is Saturn and helpful stones are amber and citrine.

This chakra controls anger and can be reactivated and rebalanced by the color yellow, the note E and the *bija mantra* Ram. The assertions that purify it are:

I now use visualization of the color yellow and the seed-sound *Rammmm...* sung on note E to act beneficially on my emotional consciousness. I use my inner power to balance my will and my feelings. I no longer take my fellow humans' words and gestures as personal attacks. I know that there are no "bad people" in this world but only "suffering people." I forgive. If, in the past, I have been hurt by someone's words or gestures, I now choose to feel the hurt one last time and I admit that it exists. Then, I let it melt into the universe, carried by the vibrations of the color yellow and by the sound Ram. I gradually feel the pain go away. I breathe the color yellow and I am absorbed in the chant of Ram. The pain disappears and I feel stronger. I am the master of my emotions. I am the master of my will. I am aware of my own power. I am the immortal *atma*, indestructible and eternally happy. I am of divine essence. I am one with God in quality.

4. THE CONSCIOUSNESS-CENTER OF AIR (*ANAHATA CHAKRA*)

This is the heart's lotus. In Sanskrit, anahata means a sound created without being generated by physical action—like a musical instrument that is not blown, not beaten, not strummed. This electromagnetic center is linked to the soul. It is through this chakra that love is felt. It corresponds to the energetic center

 of love. If we direct this love toward the inferior chakras, we *fall* in love and when these centers are unbalanced, love is tainted with egoism, possession and jealousy, blocking the elevation of the soul. If, on the contrary, we direct it toward the higher chakras, we *rise* in love and chances are that this feeling will become beneficial, particularly if it is devoid of judgment and guilt, and open to unlimited states of consciousness.

The chakra of the heart harmonizes with the color green, the note F and the seed-sound Yam. Upset, it provokes asthma, cardiac disorders, hypertension and other health problems. Stones such as pink quartz, tourmaline and emeralds are particularly favorable to this chakra. It corresponds to the air and is influenced by the planet Venus. The metal it is most sensitive to is copper. During reharmonization of this *chakra,* it is good to burn lavender or jasmine because these herbs vibrate in perfect harmony with the energies it holds within it.

Assertions for the center of the heart are:

> It is necessary and urgent that the unique experience of spiritual sound vibration be experienced everywhere in the world; this experience triggers a profound change in the hearts of individuals.

I breathe the color green and I chant the sound *Yanimm...* on the note F. I feel that these vibrations strengthen my immune system. I now realize that I feel love for all types of people, independent of their condition, race, situation or exterior appearance. I feel genuine love for them. I feel grateful for all of humanity. The more I give, the more I receive. I feel that these vibrations and energies strengthen my whole body and brighten my mind. I feel that pure and unconditional love permeates my entire self. I feel my heart opening. I am capable of giving but also of receiving. I now visualize the person that I wish to love unconditionally. This relationship is my strength and my joy. I am the receptacle and the source of love. From my heart, a river of light shoots forth and irrigates the entire Earth. I am of divine essence, immortal. I am at one with God and I am at one with His love. I receive this love and spontaneously return it to all living beings.

5. THE CONSCIOUSNESS-CENTER OF SOUND (*VISUDDHA CHAKRA*)

This is the center of ether. Only sound can penetrate ether and for this reason the *visuddha chakra* is the transmitter and receiver of sound. It is located just behind the throat and is directly related to the thyroid gland. When congested with negativity, the symptoms are easily identified: a sore throat, a stiff neck, a cold, ear problems and disorders of the thyroid gland. It is influenced by the planets Neptune and Mercury. Its activating stone is turquoise. This is the chakra of communication, expression, and judgment. It expresses itself through the voice. Its color is blue, its note G and its *bija mantra* Ham. Assertions freeing it from its blockages are:

I visualize this person with whom I cannot fully communicate (whether it is someone from my family, a friend or a business contact is of little importance). The energetic vibrations of the color blue, the note G, and the sound *Hammmm...* now help me to express what I feel. Moreover, I can express the slightest details of my life without keeping secrets. Thus, I feel how good it is to express myself. Words flow easily and I feel no tension. My throat opens, unknots itself and I feel that from now on, I am able to say everything I have always wished I could say.

I remember having been judgmental of my

fellow human beings. I hear again each word, each thought. I then feel the blue energy and the sound vibration Ham liberating me from all these judgments and words. I communicate my enthusiasm to others and I know everyone understands me. I am free to express everything I feel within. I am free of judgment and everyone understands my positive attitude. I am the free expression of God. I am the soul eternally free to communicate and express all the details of my divine life.

6. THE CONSCIOUSNESS-CENTER OF LIGHT (*ajna chakra*)

The third eye, or consciousness-center of light, is located on the forehead. In Sanskrit, *ajna* means, "command." From this third eye springs the thought-forms at the origin of all developments on the screen of life. Human beings are thus endowed with the most extraordinary instrument of creation. They can visualize what they desire and this image will manifest in their existence. There is no vision without light. It is through this center that we possess the divine power to obtain everything we choose to imagine, consciously or unconsciously. If we can imagine something, we can obtain and reach it. Through *ajna chakra* everything we wish for ourselves or for our brothers and sisters is realized. Through *ajna chakra,* we are the command, the authority giving its orders to the circumstances of life. By directing this center, we genuinely become masters. We are no longer meek victims resigned in the face of the events of existence.

The color of this chakra is indigo (dark blue with red or violet undertones). Its note is A and its *bija mantra om*. It influences the pineal gland. Its improper functioning provokes blindness, headaches, and nightmares. The planet Jupiter influences it and its metal is silver. The stone related to the third eye is quartz crystal. The assertions influencing this chakra are:

> I now concentrate on something I truly desire (it can be something material or spiritual). I visualize this thing in the color indigo, making it vibrate to the sound *Ommmm...* on the note A. I imagine this object, this situation or this circumstance in its every detail. I touch it through creative imagination, I feel its very surface, I breathe its perfume, I appreciate its exact forms with the help of my subtle vision; I hear its sounds. Now, I project this vision into the world. I feel that this image becomes reality in all its splendor and I am overwhelmed with joy. I know that everything I can dream of or imagine becomes a reality.
>
> I visualize what I genuinely want to do with my life, with my destiny. I visualize my dearest desire in all its details, aromas, forms, colors, sounds, and I project it into the world. I am the creator of my circumstances. No one else but myself is responsible for the events marking my existence. Everything I conceive becomes reality. I am of divine essence. I am qualitatively one with God.

7. THE CONSCIOUSNESS-CENTER OF BEYOND (SAHASRARA CHAKRA)

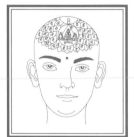

This *chakra* is also known as *brahmarandra*. *Randra* means opening. This passage gives us access to *Brahman,* the spiritual plane. It is the door to heaven, located just above the head on the subtle body. It opens into the realm beyond time and space. Its color is violet, the last in the solar spectrum. It vibrates to the note B and its *bija mantra* consists of all the sound frequencies connected with the Divine Names; these Names culminate in the *mahavakya* or *mahamantra* A.U.M., which is the complete representation of the Divine and everything that is.

This magnetic center is related to the pituitary gland. When it is congested, the physical body and the mind react with depression, madness, boredom or the incapacity to face life. It is influenced by the planet Uranus, its metal is gold and its beneficial stone is the diamond or, even more so, the amethyst. Its reactivating assertions follow:

> I now visualize God as I conceive Him. This image is held above my head, bathed in the color violet. I feel that this divine image enters into me and

I integrate it. I let the three sacred letters A.U.M. make all the elements of my being vibrate.

A is the Father, U is the Divine Mother, and M, all living creatures and all that is. Now, I visualize God and all that is and let the visualization carry me beyond my own understanding. Further and further, closer and closer. God is omnipresent. I let the divine image carry me where it wishes, in the outer world as well as the inner world in form and formlessness. The omnipresence becomes presence. This presence is within me. It is a part of myself and I am a part of it. It illuminates each of my chakras. All colors, all sounds become one. I feel I can really rely on this presence. It is within me. It is real. It is everywhere in my life. It loves me. I know that this love relationship is infinite and absolute. I am perfectly loved. I am the immortal soul, eternally happy.

This reharmonization exercise of the astral body can be practiced every day. Try it in the morning to charge up with good frequencies and at night to connect with cosmic energies in order to regain physical and subtle strength. Like Hermes, let us not forget that everything is vibration, nothing is inert, everything vibrates, everything is balanced by compensating oscillations; all cause has an effect, all effect has a cause, everything has a masculine and feminine principle, everything has two poles, everything is spirit. The human body is a sound box, a musical instrument that, like any other instrument, should be regularly tuned. Such a technical *tuning* ensures that we know a state of health, peace and unforgettable joy.

HEALING THROUGH THE SUN MANTRA

All the mantric forces represent an appeal. In other words, these sound formulas are used to obtain something. Sometimes, sounds act directly on matter. At other times, the mantra is addressed to the force of divinity that presides over a particular physical element. The *om ghrami suryay namah* or sun mantra, for instance, is sung when a serious illness appears. It is practiced while the sun is half raised. Patients stand facing the sun's rays, holding in their right hand a copper pot filled with pure water. They then offer the water to the sun and chant the mantra—*om ghrami suryay namah*—three times. Afterwards, it is recommended that the mantra be sung as often as one wishes, until the patient is cured.

This purification ritual is mentioned in a very ancient book entitled *Aditya Hriday,* given in Sanskrit by Krishna to Samb, one of his sons, who at the time was suffering from an incurable illness. After a while of using this practice, Samb was cured. Ramesh Chandra Jyotishi, also known as Mauna Baba, an astrologer from Vrindavan, India, recounted the story of this very special mantra to me.

There are mantras suited to all needs. In addition to those that bring health, others bring wealth or protection. The list is infinite and there are as many mantric possibilities as there are desires in the human heart. We will see, however, that the most liberating mantras are those diametrically opposed to the requests of the ego. These are mantras that do not represent requests but which, passed down from one disciple to the next, are formed by

God's revealed names, under the multiple characteristics of the Absolute Being, and sung in an altogether spontaneous manner.

THE HEALING NAMES OF GOD

Of all known mantras, the "mantras of the names," or Holy Names, are the most powerful because they are surrounded with the halo of the pure light of love, and the soul that sings them expects nothing in return. Reciting them is a celebratory act of devotion. The song of Holy Names is not the result of a particular calculation, or of bargaining with divine forces. These mantras correspond to a spontaneous feeling that springs from the depths of the heart.

Nearly all great thinkers in the fields of visualization and creative assertion are unanimous in saying that the spoken word is much more powerful when it is pronounced in a state of thanks or acknowledgment for what has already been received, rather than calling attention to a perceived deficiency. To wish or appeal for health, for example, proves to the subconscious that the body does not possess it and that consequently it lacks it. In no way can a lack create a fulfillment. Any lacking inevitably results in greater lacking. As success leads to success, the feeling of emptiness or lack of something actually pro-

> Genuine security rests on one thing only: the harmonization of the subtle body.

vokes a state of emptiness. Similarly, the vibrating waves radiating from a feeling of fright inevitably lead to the events at the origin of such a feeling. Fearing something is the best way to ensure that the dreaded event takes place. Feeling the reality of a set of circumstances unfailingly results in that reality. Thus, the true positive and creative assertion is not a request or a question but a response corresponding to a feeling of plenitude.

In the practice of the Holy Names, the same law applies. This is why singing the Holy Names is not done as prayer, as a prayer most often involves a petition. In opposition to this state of solicitation, the Holy Names are free. Without supplication, the song provides a limitless joy inexpressible in human language. The soul that practices such a song—regardless of the particular name it feels attracted to or the system of thought it draws inspiration from—does not demand anything, does not implore, does not beg, and does not solicit. From its lips comes a song of joy, which does not command or give orders. The only desire remains the desire to stay in the ecstatic presence of the name, for the vibration of the living light is absolutely no different from God. Due to this nondifferentiation, which renders them inseparable from the absolute, the Holy Names hold inconceivable spiritual powers.

At the physical level and in a material sense, the name is different from the form. As noted previously, language—whose function it is to express thought and serve as a communications link between humans—is simply a symbolic representation. Vocal and graphic signs represent a given object or person but do not incarnate the reality they seek to evoke, imitate or replace. We have seen that they serve in building "bridges" of harmonic resonance between the person who pronounces them and the objects and beings they represent. We could say that they are the ambassadors of reality, but they are only its symbols. The word water is not the element water; it only links us harmonically to water.

On the contrary, in the realm of the Holy Names, the symbol incarnates the reality. This is why, according to Vedic thought, the divine name is the sound incarnation of the divine principle. Essential information is found on its sovereign effectiveness in all holy scriptures such as the Bible, the Koran and the Torah. But it is probably in the Vedic scriptures that references to multiple Absolute frequencies are the most numerous and the most precise.

The manner in which the Holy Names manifest a unique energy in their state of nondifferentiation is explained in the *Padma Purana*: "The Holy Names provide limitless joy to the souls who sing them. They grant all spiritual blessings, because they are God Himself, the cosmic reservoir of ultimate pleasure. These Names are complete in themselves and represent the perfect form of all peace and of all transcendental maturity. They do not correspond to a material sound or name under any condition whatsoever, and they are no less powerful than the Source of all cosmic energies. Unsoiled by material vibrations, they are never involved in the games of illusion. Free and absolute, they are never conditioned by the laws of physical nature."

The acclaimed 17th century Vaishnava poet, Narottam, wrote, "*golokera prema-dhana hari-nama sankirtana*."[70] Roughly translated, it means, "Transcendental sound vibrations have no other origin than the world of permanence, the spiritual realm." Two hundred years prior, the avatar Chaitanya sang in the verses of his *Siksastakam*: "O sublime intelligence, Your innumerable names are vested with all good fortune for the universe's living entities. Of names, You have an unlimited number, and through them, You expand into the infinite. Moreover, each of these names is charged with a specific and all-powerful energy."

Therefore, the different sound frequencies used to name the cosmic reality are not composed of ordinary syllables or sounds. These sounds originate in the other world, a world located beyond the material atmosphere. The divine nature of the Holy Name remains, however, a total mystery for those who approach it only through logic and intellectual reasoning. Only those for whom it is possible to surpass all concepts and all prejudice, who involve themselves directly in the practice of the song in a humble state of mind, without disdain nor pride, but with trust and love, will understand and fully enjoy the ecstasy of the supreme sound.

> Listening to the sacred sound vibrations linked to the Holy Names is thus the simplest means of reaching a superior plane of existence.

Invisible radio waves travel from one place to another and can be heard when an electronic receiver catches them. In the same manner, spiritual waves can be perceived and assimilated by the entity equipped with the qualities required to receive them: a peaceful consciousness and a heart open to pure love. Furthermore, hunger for freedom and the taste for experiment will greatly benefit the person who chooses to follow this path.

AT THE INSTANT OF LEAVING THE BODY

The Bible of Christians, the Koran of Muslims, the Torah of Hebrews, the Vedic scriptures of the Hindus and all books serving to enlighten humankind are unanimous on one major point: the divine principle—regardless of its name, aspect or the actions attributed to God—is the source of all entities. Therefore, living beings are subproducts of an all-powerful seed, regardless of the culture, tradition, religion or region of the world with which they identify in this present life. In addition, these subproducts possess the same qualitative potential as their creator. Jesus asserted this truth two thousand years ago in Matthew 5.48: "Be perfect as your Heavenly Father is perfect."

The Vedic scriptures teach that the individual spirit soul is simultaneously, inconceivably one and different from the Absolute *(achintyabhedabheda tattva)*. As a part and parcel of the complete and absolute whole, the divine spiritual spark possesses its qualities. Eternity *(sat)*, consciousness *(chit)* and happiness *(ananda)* are therefore the supra-natural heritage of all entities. The sole difference between the cosmic soul and the soul is quantitative, although at the level of the Absolute, essence is everything.

From time immemorial, living entities have chosen

to experience life with the goal of directing and control-
ling creation as they pleased. This is why we clothe ourselves in a physical body, which serves us as a vehicle for
a few earthly years. After a while, this ephemeral body re-
turns to the elements and, consequently, the living being
leaves it to take on a new body. The forms and qualities
of this new vehicle of flesh are determined by the activities, desires and memories gathered in the course of the
soul's life in the previous body. On this topic, the second
chapter of the Bhagavad Gita is once again very clear:
"At the instant of death, the soul takes on a new body as
naturally as it has passed, in the previous one, from child-
hood to youth and then to old age. This change does not
trouble the one who is aware of his true nature. Know that
what penetrates the whole body cannot be destroyed. No
one can destroy the imperishable soul. Only the bodies
it borrows are subject to destruction. The soul does not
die with the body. Living, it will never cease to be. At the
instant of death it clothes itself with a new body, as easily as one throws away old garments to put on new ones,
because the other body is now useless."[71]

Later in the same text, we find the following fundamental information:

yam yam vapi smaram bhavam
tyajaty ante kalevaram
tam tam evaity kauneteya
sada tad bhava-bhavitah

The human being's thoughts and memories at
the instant of leaving the body determine its future condition.[72]

It is therefore possible to modify one's condition at the critical moment of physical death. The question is one of knowing how to leave the body, or *die*, in the desired mental condition. Our thoughts at the moment of death are mainly determined by the sum of our actions and thoughts over the course of our entire life. These actions and thoughts are themselves determined by singing and listening to words, music and all the sound waves that constantly permeate our subconscious. The sound vibrations perceived in the present determine our future condition! Thus, spiritually absorbed in the inner enlightenment acquired by listening to the Holy Names and pure universal music, in the course of our life, we will be able to acquire, while leaving our actual bodily envelope, a spiritual and eternal body, conscious of and happy in a different molecular structure. Listening to the sacred sound vibrations linked to the Holy Names is thus the simplest means of reaching a superior plane of existence.

> In all civilizations and in all initiations, we find the assurance that sound—in particular the absolute sound of the names correlating to the Divine—represents the most powerful of transformative energies known throughout creation.

Hypnotized and narrowly conditioned by matter's atmosphere, the living being is literally submerged in a world of dreams and illusions that are never the fruit of so-called luck. Quite the contrary, they are mainly its own inclinations, thoughts and memories. For the living being, this hypnotic condition of death and rebirth *(saṁsāra)* corresponds on one hand to the oblivion of the original source, and on the other hand, to a state of chronic torpor into which the soul has gradually fallen while losing, from one birth to the next, the awareness of its inherent serenity, of its constitutional eternity and of its prodigious celestial origin.

This state of torpor, comparable to a deep sleep, is at the origin of the tragedy of materialistic civilizations and empires, which, through sheer ignorance of reality, base their knowledge on imperfect sensory observation, their monetary equilibrium on a totally inconsequential interpretation of Earth's wealth, and their happiness on a laborious, ungrateful and dangerous stimulation of the senses.

This way of life is very risky. Indeed, under the laws governing the universe, these societies can never lay the blame on extenuating circumstances and they are irremediably swept away on the waves of time. Thus, atheist civilizations, that is to say, civilizations in discord with the fundamental harmonics of the universe, regularly disappear from the face of the Earth, as they are so far removed from the genuine values of existence. The fall and destruction of great materialistic empires, which unfortunately mark the history of the world, correspond to the deep sleep of the conditioned soul that painfully persists in searching for life on paths leading only to death.

Wanting to acquire happiness by doing things that only aim to satisfy mental and sensual needs is the worst of errors for the soul. It is urgent we understand that the world can only survive if humans awaken to the truth of the soul. Any other consideration, whether economical or political, will draw the planet even further into alienation, war, savagery and finally, annihilation.

waking up the one who sleeps

What will satisfy the fish out of water? Certainly it will only be content when it is put back in the stream. Similarly, nothing perfectly satisfies human beings but the spiritual sound vibration that is actually their eternal element. The individual soul is a particle of the universal soul. Its cosmic position consists in living, loving and working spontaneously in harmony with the galaxy as a whole. However, it is prevented from doing so by the state of chronic sleep in which it has foundered. Therefore, each of us has the mission of awakening within ourselves this marvelous spark that has lain dormant for so long. Such is the true goal of our human lives, before dreams and illusions carry us toward further difficulty.

It is universally recognized that sound has the power to draw the consciousness out of sleep, to awaken it. Who has not experienced the ringing of an alarm clock? Along the same lines, the soul asleep in the bed of the physical world can awaken to real life through spiritual sound vibration. This vibration is mainly present in the sound of the Holy Names designating the essential cosmic principle. It is buried there, hidden away; nonetheless we can perceive it through the practice of listening and singing these potent names.

Five hundred years ago Chaitanya taught, "*nam-nam akari bahu-dha nija-sarva-saktis*," or "The sound vibration of Your name can alone, O Lord, overwhelm the soul with all graces. Of sublime names, You possess an infinite number, vested with all spiritual powers. No strict rules must be followed to sing them." This is not new, of course. Thousands of years ago, the illustrious Gita mentioned the sacred nature of the singing and hearing of the Holy Names: "Among the sound vibrations I am *om,* the absolute syllable, and among the means to spiritual realization, I am the *japa,* the song of sacred names."[73]

The Bible itself instructs, "Whoever invokes the Name of the Lord will be saved." The Psalms describe the means by which the soul is liberated from material contingencies: "May the sons of Zion praise the name of Yahweh through dance and song."

This divine sound vibration that holds the power to awaken the sleeping soul is the eternal *shabda-brahma.* Originally, the *shabda-brahma* was composed of names, acts, attributes and qualities of the highest reality. *Shabda* is, as we have heard, the original inner sound. It is this nonmaterial vibration that enjoys the power to liberate the sleeping forces ensconced within us since the dawn of time. We are all the heirs and holders of these subtle energies. The awakening of these energies can be manifested by means of this mystical force.

Thus awakened, our subtle energies disentangle the centers of our ethereal bodies and unknot the electromagnetic points rendered sterile and inert by an art of living in opposition to the universe's rhythm. The spiritual sound vibration makes the self's whole interior vibrate harmoniously. This unique force is capable of healing the illnesses inherent in the realm of illusion.

a song filled with peace

It will be necessary for the human being to learn how to use sound if he wishes to participate in any way in the divine work. The first magical manifestation will then be the incantation. The priest—of whatever religious persuasion—will be the priest "accurate of voice" of Egyptian tradition, or the Indian singer, or the solar hero of mythology, the great Hermes whose song attracted to him animals drunk with joy.[74]

— Anne Osmont, *Rhythm: Creator of Forces and Forms*

One of the most beautiful fruits of the music of the soul is the eradication of anxiety. The means of expression and the singer's motivation are essential in obtaining a sensitive effect. Human and universal pacification is the sacred song in itself when it is held within the singer's intent. The song can therefore set free all its strength, not merely touching exterior things, but also the inner rhythms of the universe. At this level of understanding, sound becomes a vibration comparable to a type of magnetism acting on the secret nature of human beings much more effectively than on visible organs. Herein also lies the power of mantras. The incantatory chant, rhythmical and sung, is *charged* with the intent of the individual who makes it vibrate. At this moment, it is irresistible.

The *Gandharva Veda*, the book of the celestial singer, is a veritable treatise on sacred song and mystical music. A great number of its songs can lead the initiate to certain states of ecstasy. To express their power, recall the story of the Ramayana. In it Ravana, the fiend who kidnapped Sita from Rama (but failed to seduce her because genuine love is impenetrable), incurs Shiva's anger with his audacity. Only one glance from Shiva was enough to reduce the presumptuous villain to dust. Ravana suddenly remembered the "song that appeases anger" and, evoking it, sent peace and unconditional love into the heart of the angered god, and thus obtained his forgiveness.

It is enough to relax muscle tension, to breathe deeply and, while visualizing a peaceful image, to slowly

repeat the word *shanti* (peace), preceded and followed by the syllable *om,* to genuinely feel the most extraordinary of sensations: peace.

Krishnadas Kaviraj's *Sri Chaitanya Charitamrita* tells the story of Chaitanya Mahaprabhu, who, like Hermes and his transformative lyre, could charm wild animals with only the sound of his voice. The text relates that one day Mahaprabhu was crossing the jungle of Kataka in Bengal, completely absorbed in the singing of the 32 syllable mantra composed of the Holy Names of Krishna, Rama and Hare. Attracted by the sound of his voice, the many tigers haunting the jungle at the time surrounded him, though without antagonism. When Balabhadra Bhattacharya, Mahaprabhu's companion, saw him touch one of the tigers with his foot, he was petrified with terror. But the tiger's attitude surprised him even more. The animal raised himself onto his back paws and began to roar in delight. It then began to dance to the rhythm of the mantra, bewitched by Mahaprabhu's soft voice.

In all civilizations and in all initiations, we find the assurance that sound—in particular the absolute sound of the names correlating to the Divine—represents the most powerful of transformative energies known throughout creation.

GOD as SOUND: a MULTITUDe OF names FOR a SINGLe essence

The preceding anecdote shows just how power-ful the 32-syllable mantra (the *mahamantra*, or great mantra) can be. In fact, the ancient *Pura-nas* describe this mantra as being "God as sound," simi-lar to the A.U.M. vibration. Therefore, it is not surprising that sung with a perfectly pure heart, it has the power to make wild animals dance. The chant of this mantra is so powerful that even trees and plants respond to it! What can be said, then, of its effect on human beings?

In another story from that time, Haridasa, the ac-knowledged master of chanting the Holy Names, is asked how trees and plants can be freed from the bondage of samsara. Haridasa answered that singing the *maha-mantra* aloud is not only of invaluable help to the souls presently incarnated as plants, but also beneficial to in-sects and to all living beings. The extraordinary power of the *mahamantra* comes from its divine origin. A gift of saints and sages, this category of elevated sound vi-bration has appeared in our world consistently over the course of thousands of years.

In *Sri Chaitanya Shikshamrita,* Bhaktivinode Thakur, one of India's finest poet-philosophers, clearly ex-plains why the superficial differences existing between the sacred names of the great religions are, in fact, of no importance whatsoever. According to Bhaktivinode, al-though human nature is the same everywhere, people liv-ing in different countries and on different continents ac-quire various secondary characteristics. It is impossible to find within this world two people with the same secondary nature. If we can observe different personalities and appearances in two brothers born of the same mother, then it is natural to note a disparity between humans born in different regions of the globe.

In different countries, phenomena such as the location of waterways, the movements of air masses, mountains, forests and the quantity of available food and clothing all show marked variations. Consequently, certain differences naturally appear in physiognomy, social positioning, activity, music, religion, styles of clothing and food preferences. As each nationality has a particular way of viewing life, various conceptions of reality seem superficially to be opposed, but they are of the same essence. What seems to be opposed is the name each nation, each people, gives to the universal divine principle.

> In spite of the five primary differences that distinguish the religions of the world, we should recognize all processes of purification and acceleration whose goal is attaining devotion to all aspects of the Divine (*bhakti*) as truthful.

Just as in different places people awaken from their primitive condition and gradually develop culture, science, laws and devotion for the universal substance, their adoration is also divergent in vocabulary, customs, offerings, music and inner attitude. If we consider all these apparent disparities from an impartial point of view, however, we will encounter no contradiction, no evil, as long as the object of adoration remains the same. It is therefore appropriate to sing our inspired meditative or mantric song, without ever ridiculing the meditative methods of others.

Why should a Christian go to war with a Muslim?

Why should a Buddhist judge a Hindu? All human beings are seekers in the immense cosmos and they sense the same energy simultaneously and inconceivably, personally and impersonally at the same time. Therefore, they should unite their efforts, their testimonies and their research. In the light of the factors mentioned previously, systems that elevate consciousness and that are applied throughout the world present five major differences:

1. Different spiritual masters
2. Different emotional states linked to meditation
3. Different rituals
4. Different affections and activities with regard to the focus of concentration
5. Different terminologies and appellations resulting from use of different languages.

In keeping with the variety of revealed guides and texts, in some regions people honor the sages of Vedic culture, in other places, they revere Mohammed and his prophets, and in other regions still, they are attached to the holy individuals who follow the teachings of Jesus. Similarly, each locality shows a particular respect for different philosophers. Each community should, of course, honor its own spiritual masters, guides or teachers, but none should try to prove the superiority of its master's instructions under the pretext of acquiring a great number of followers. The propagation of such antagonistic positions is disastrous!

With regard to adoration, prescribed rituals vary according to the individual's devotional sentiments and mentality. In certain areas, spiritualists sit in a place

of power, where they practice renunciation and breath control. Elsewhere, they prostrate themselves five times a day in the direction of their master's tomb in order to offer their praise without worry over the situation they are in. Yet elsewhere, they kneel in the temple or in their homes, hands joined, and acknowledge the indestructibility of the soul while glorifying the Divine.

Each type of adoration differs in clothing, food, rules of cleanliness and so forth. Moreover, the feeling and the conduct toward the adored *object* vary from religion to religion. Certain devotees, their consciousness saturated with devotion, install a form of God in their hearts, in their thoughts or on an altar. Other processes, more inclined to logical reasoning, completely reject the external image. Hence, initiates must create a concept of God in their minds and adore it. Nevertheless, we should realize that *all* deities—concrete, abstract, visible or invisible—described in the various scriptures are, in reality, authentic representations of the Absolute.

Above all, it is important to grasp that different languages give the Absolute various names. Religious systems also have different names and they have given an appropriate appellation to each object of worship. Because of the five general differences previously mentioned, a great number of the world's religions have developed very differently from one another. These differences should not be the source of mutual disagreements, however, because this leads to disaster.

If, at the hour of prayer, we find ourselves in the temple of a religious group different from ours, we should think: Here, the Absolute is worshipped in a new way. It is referred to by a name different from the one I know. It is not obligatory that I participate in this ritual. However, this scene creates within me a more intense feeling for my own meditation. Absolute truth is one. Therefore, I offer my praise to the form I see here and I pray to the Infinite (from which this "form" is born) that this particular deity help me increase my love for Him.

> Likewise, the transcendental nature of the Name cannot be known other than by direct experimentation. It is not a question of believing, but of doing.

Those who do not act in this way, but who show malice or envy or who ridicule other meditative processes, certainly deviate from true spirituality, thus proving their lack of universal vision. When these people truly elevate their vibratory frequencies through one process or another, this sort of useless quarrel will no longer attract them. Pure love *(prema)*, in fact, incarnates the eternal religion of the spiritual soul *(sanatana dharma)*, and hence, in spite of the five primary differences that distinguish the religions of the world, we should recognize all processes of purification and acceleration whose goal is attaining devotion to all aspects of the Divine *(bhakti)* as truthful.

It is useless to quarrel over a name or engage in trivial dissension. The value of a method of self-realization cannot only be *judged* by the purity of the goal it is aimed at reaching. Reading the thoughts of Bhaktivinode Thakur, one grasps all the futility, all the extreme ignorance and all the formidable hypocrisy that lead men to kill one another in the name of a particular God! We understand  once and for all that so-called religious wars are, in fact, wars of power and profit fueled by the greed and the savagery of a few regressive individuals disguised as religious leaders. Unfortunately, still today they find hordes of unscrupulous followers.

SINGING THE SACRED NAMES

It is not necessary to adopt an official religion to progress spiritually or to practice singing the Holy Names. Certain people, to whom the term "revealed" means nothing and the Latin word *religare* (to link oneself with the Absolute) remains enigmatic, cannot find resonance with any scripture. For many, God is dead or simply an abstraction, a dream or a utopia. Not having met an *acharya*, or living master who teaches by example, conditioned as they are by family and society, these people haven't made the effort to seek further. They have simply accepted, without personal investigation, mundane ideas put forth by the majority. Without really knowing why, they have reached the conclusion that an omnipresent supernatural power cannot exist in a world where war, obscurity and hatred are rampant.

An alien landing in the middle of a desert would not see any trace of water and thereby make the same kind of error by concluding that water cannot exist on Earth. The calamities and misfortunes of creation do not necessarily imply the absence of a creator. The happiness and misfortune of humans is only the rightful reward of their words, actions, thoughts and music.

Be this as it may, it is not a matter of believing or not, but rather of doing, of experiencing and *tasting*. Whether or not the word "God" has meaning for us, there is no need for us to change our way of seeing things before beginning this practice. The seeker who has not yet experienced the revelation of the inner presence can just as easily start the work of transformation with a simple supposition—the idea of God as a working hypothesis. Is not supposition, after all, the method most commonly employed in pure science?

Whatever our convictions, it is always possible to choose a sound vibration composed of one of the recognized frequencies and to use it to our benefit. What is important is to sing the Name, regardless of what tradition it belongs to. As noted, to attempt the experiment of the experience of the Name, it is not even necessary to believe in a superior intelligence.

Sit comfortably, in a secluded place, breathe deeply and relax. Let your mind wander without fighting it, as you would let the water flow in a river, and simply, naturally, experience the Name. To listen is all that is necessary.

From the lips, the sound travels to the ears and descends into the heart. The activity of the senses and mind then seems to stop and we experience a happiness that no language is able to describe. We feel peace and joy saturated with the beauty of life. We discover the wonderful melody of genuine love. This primordial vibration has the power to liberate us from the cycle of death and rebirth by setting us on the road home, toward peace and light. Although it is simple, it is nonetheless a practice that is refined over time.

As we have seen, a mantra is a sound structure whose modulations hold a proven power. Often formed from the Sanskrit alphabet's fifty signs—the *Devanagari,* or language of the gods—the mantra allows the mind to concentrate. Most mantras used for meditation are chosen from among the multiple names corresponding to the primary source. The repetition of such mantras is called *japa.* A great many masters have corroborated the Vedic science by emphasizing that japa is especially recommended for our present age as an effective means of self-realization. The *Sri Chaitanya Charitamrita* states: "In the present age of Kali the chanting of the Holy Names, japa, represents the true technique for reaching enlightenment." In fact, japa is called the *yuga dharma*, or the means of reaching salvation, the *dharma* of every living being in this particular cosmic cycle, the *Kali Yuga.*

Chanting and listening are easy methods that can be practiced by people of all ages. If we do not feel any particular attraction for one Holy Name, or if we prefer a specific Holy Name, we need only choose the one most suited to us. For instance, if the name Rama or Krishna doesn't appeal for one reason or another, practice singing the name of Christ, Allah, Jehovah, Yahwe, Adonais or Buddha.

Consequently, even though we are of a given religious persuasion, whether we consider ourselves Hindu,

כֹהת	אכא	לֹלה	מֹהש	עֹלם	סיט	יֹלי	והֹו
הֹקם	הרי	מבה	יֹזל	ההע	לאו	אלד	הֹזי
וזהֹו	מֹלה	יֹיי	נֹלך	פֹהל	לוו	כֹלי	לאו
וֹשׁר	לכב	אום	רֹיי	שֹׁאה	ירת	האא	נתה
יֹיז	רֹהע	וֹזעם	אֹני	מֹנֹד	כוק	לֹהֹוֹ	יֹוו
מֹיה	עֹעֹל	עֹרי	סֹאל	ילֹה	וֹול	מֹיכ	הֹהֹה
פֹוי	מבֹה	נֹית	נֹנא	עֹמם	הֹוֹזֹע	דֹני	והֹו
מֹוֹזי	עֹנֹו	יֹהה	וֹמב	מֹצֹר	הֹרֹוז	יֹיֹל	נֹמם
מֹום	הֹיֹי	יֹבֹמ	רֹאה	וֹזֹבֹו	אֹיֹע	מֹנֹק	דֹמב

Christian, Buddhist or Muslim, we can easily commit to the practice of the Name as outlined in the spiritual message we are inclined by education, culture or tradition to accept. To be free from religious identifications, however, it is necessary to develop a connection with our inner guide, the lord of the heart.

As it's possible to learn mathematics at any university, one can develop love for God by following any authentic path. Thus, the Name in itself matters little. What is important is to sing it or to listen to it. Singing and listening allow us to experience the very nature of the Name. We taste the immortal nectar. No word is worthy of describing this unforgettable experience. One can, for instance, write pages about the nature of honey, analyze the elements composing the substance, and point out that honey is sweet, smooth and flavorful. But no explanation, no book or lecture can replace the direct experience of honey. You must taste it to *know* it.

Likewise, the transcendental nature of the Name cannot be known other than by direct experimentation. It is not a question of believing, but of doing. There is no worldly barrier to the singing of the Name. A Muslim can sing the name of Allah; a Christian, that of Christ; a Hindu, that of Rama, Krishna or Narayan; a Buddhist, that of Buddha. Nor is it necessary to be rich or poor, learned or simple. It costs nothing: the song of the Name is free. It can be practiced anywhere, under any circumstances, alone or with others. Everyone can sing it and draw the greatest benefit from this universal practice. For this singing and listening, no stringent rules exist.

The singing of the Name is recommended in Biblical scriptures. The Psalms urge us to sing and glorify it: "All nations that You have created will come before Thee, O Lord, and will glorify Thy Name." Chronicles, in the Old Testament, gives us further steadfast advice: "Give thanks unto the Lord, call upon his name,  make known his deeds among the people; sing unto him, sing psalms unto him, talk ye of all his wondrous works; glory ye in his holy name: let the heart of them rejoice that seek the Lord."

In Romans, Saint Paul adds: "For there is no difference between the Jew and the Greek, for the same Lord over all is rich unto all that call upon him; for whosoever shall call upon the name of the Lord shall be saved." And Jesus relates the same message in John 17:6, when he says, "I have manifested thy name unto the men which thou gavest me out of the world: thine they were, and thou gavest them me; and they have kept thy word." Thus Jesus taught his followers to pray: "Our Father, who art in heaven, hallowed be Thy Name."

Like instrumentalists who practice scales and arpeggios daily, or composers, who want their music to touch the hearts of their audience, it is also possible to meditate daily on the essential realities of the universe.

We have the opportunity to regularly exercise our mental powers to the arpeggios of peace, beauty, truth and benevolence. So let our daily exercise be active meditation. Let our scales be composed of the sounds of the Infinite, according to the tradition that attracts us.

> Singing the Name has always been recognized as a means of authentic and effective realization. When we come into contact with electricity, we feel its energy, regardless of the line through which it passes.

One may concentrate more specifically on the mantra received from their personal guide during initiation; there are numerous words of power issued from a variety of spiritual traditions. Singing the Name has always been recognized as a means of authentic and effective realization. When we come into contact with electricity, we feel its energy, regardless of the line through which it passes.

THE HOLY names
OF various TRADITIONS

Holy Names According to Islam

Allahu Akbar
La Ilah Ill' Allahu
Bishmillah Ir-Rahman Ir-Rahim
Allah, Allah

The prophet Mohammed is often quoted as saying, "The hour of death will not take by surprise he who sings the name of the Lord."

Holy Names According to Christianity

Lord Jesus Christ
Jesus, Jesus
Holy Mary, mother of God

Holy Names According to Hinduism

Om Namo Bhagavate Vasudevaya
Sri Ram, Jai Ram, Jai Jai Ram
Hari Om
Hare Krishna, Hare Krishna,
Krishna Krishna, Hare Hare,
Hare Rama, Hare Rama,
Rama Rama, Hare Hare

As Hinduism consists of several primary lineages, opinions occasionally vary concerning the relative or absolute power of the many mantras found in the Vedic literature. The mantras provided herein are drawn primarily from the Vaishnava branch.

Holy Names According to Buddhism

Om Mani Padme Hūṁ
Namu Amida Buddhsu
Kwanzeon Bosatsu

The *Zendo*, a well-known Buddhist treatise written by Hakuin in the 18th century, instructs:

> Simply repeat the name of Amida with all your heart, when you are lying down or seated, when you are walking or when standing still, never cease to practice the Name, even for one instant. Such is the work that infallibly provides salvation, as it is in concordance with Buddha's original desire.
>
> The greatest medicine is the call of the name of Amida (Buddha) and this call is contained in the six syllables NA MU A MI DA BU. This chant represents the perfect concentration on the name of Buddha. To practice it, no knowledge is required. All we need do is pronounce the words and listen. In the sound of these six syllables lies the pivotal point of a fundamental power.

The names that are one with the universal necessity are all vested with the same sacred character, because they all point to the same absolute person or energy. These Holy Names have all the power of the supreme being. Nothing can thus be opposed to the fact that each of us, in whichever part of the world we reside, spontaneously sings and praises the Divine through the specific name that serves to designate it in a given area.

These names, the source of all good fortune, are not intended to be sung for the fulfillment of worldly desire, but instead out of our real necessity. For them to be genuinely effective, it is preferable to pronounce or sing them with an altruistic goal, with mind and heart turned toward the highest ideal of love. The thirst for this absolute love, provoked by the singing of the Holy Names, represents one of the most energetic means of adapting our own vibratory rate to that of the superior planes, inaccessible to the purely physical senses and powers of reasoning. Again, this mystical song can be freely practiced by anyone.

Just as there is no limit to genuine love, there are absolutely no bounds to the initiatory emotion of singing the Holy Names. Wherever we find ourselves in life, each and every one of us can find in this song the greatest well-being and the greatest benefit.

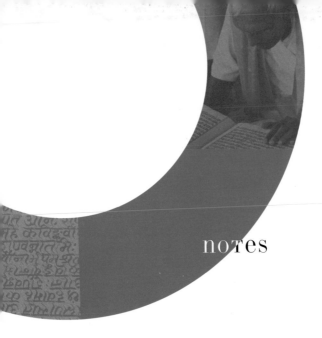

notes

In citing works in the notes, the Bhagavad Gita has been abbreviated as Bg.

[1] Cyril Scott, *Music: Its Secret Influence Through the Ages* (La musique, son influence secrète à travers les âges) (Paris: Édition de la Baconnière, 1984).

[2] See Music of the Spheres website, located at http://peyote.com/jonstef/spheres.htm

[3] Dane Rudhyar, *The Magic of Tone and the Art of Music* (La magie du ton et l'art de la musique) (Paris: Arista, 1985).

[4] *Substance Abuse in Brief,* Center for Substance Abuse Treatment, SAMHSA, U.S. Department of Health and Human Services, July 1999

[5] J. Thomas Zébério, *Sounds and Human Energy* (Les sons et l'énergie humaine) (Paris: Courrier du livre, 1979).

[6] Rolando Benenzon, *Manual of Musicotherapy* (Manuel de musicothérapie) (Toulouse, France: Édition de Privat, 1981).

[7] Ralph Tegtmeier, *Guide to New Musics for the Inner Journey* (Guide des musiques nouvelles pour le voyage intérieur) (Paris: Le Souffle d'Or, 1988).

[8] Dr. John Diamond, *Your Body Doesn't Lie* (New York, NY: Warner Books, 1980).

[9] Hal A. Lingerman, *The Healing Energies of Music* (Wheaton, IL: Theosophical Publishing House/Quest Books, 1983).

[10] Rolando Benenzon, *Manual of Musicotherapy* (Manuel de musicothérapie) (Toulouse, France: Édition de Privat, 1981).

[11] Source unknown

[12] See "Headaches: A spectrum of pain presents a dilemma for doctors" by Kathleen Phalen posted at www.ama-assn.org/amednews/2001/10/15/hlsa1015.htm

[13] From "Health Consequences and Harmful Effects of Noise," posted at www.szu.cz/chzp/repo1/szu_02an/ka02_06.htm

[14] According to a study performed by the California Institute. See www.caslpa.ca/PDF/fact%20sheets/noise%20induced%20hearing%20loss.pdf

[15] Annie Moch. *Los efectos nocivos del ruido.* Nueva Paideia, 1985.

[16] Richard Cannavo and Fred Hidalgo, in an article in *Paroles et musiques* 15 (February, 1989).

[17] Ibid.

[18] Ibid.

[19] Marie-Louise Aucher, *Sonorous Man* (L'homme sonore) (Paris: Epi, 1983).

[20] Rolando Benenzon, *Manual of Musicotherapy* (Manuel de musicothérapie) (Toulouse, France: Édition de Privat, 1981).

[21] Hélène Caya, *From Sound Springs Light* (Du son jaillit la lumière) (Montreal: Denis J. Paradis Publishers, 1987).

[22] Joe Stuessy, *Rock and Roll: As History and Stylistic Development,* (Englewood Cliffs, NJ: Prentice-Hall, Inc. 1990).

[23] Bg. 3.27

[24] Bg. 14.5

[25] Aveline and Michio Kushi, *Macrobiotic Pregnancy and Care of the Newborn* (Grossesse macrabiotique et soins au nouveau-né) (Paris: Guy Trédaniel, 1986).

[26] Chantal Drolet and Anne-Marie Sicotte, "Nutrition that Kills" (L'alimentation qui tue) *Resource Guide* 4:6 (July-August 1989).

[27] Louis Kuhne, *The New Science of Healing* (La nouvelle science de guérir) (Paris: Cevic, 1978).

[28] Dr. Paul Carton, *The Laws of Healthy Life* (Les lois de la vie saine) (Copyright by Paul Carton, 1922).

[29] Joan Gilbert provided this quote to Jon Wynne-Tyson for his book, *The Extended Circle,* published in 1985. It was excerpted from a letter Einstein had written to the publication *Vegetarian Watch-Tower*, December 27, 1930.

[30] Henry David Thoreau, *Walden,* Beacon Press edition, 1997.

[31] Ibid.

[32] Edward Podolsky, *The Doctor Prescribes Music* (New York, NY: Frederick A. Stockes, 1939).

[33] Hal A. Lingerman, *The Healing Energies of Music* (Wheaton, IL: Theosophical Publishing House/Quest Books, 1983).

[34] Edward Podolsky, *The Doctor Prescribes Music* (New York, NY: Frederick A. Stockes, 1939).

[35] Bg. 3.43

[36] Bg. 9.26

[37] Cyril Scott, *Music: Its Secret Influence Through the Ages* (La musique, son influence secrète à travers les âges) (Paris: Édition de la Baconnière, 1984).

[38] Roland de Candé, *Invitation to Music* (L'invitation à la musique) (Paris: Édition du Seuil, 1980).

[39] Mikhaël Aïvanhov, *Artistic Creation and Spiritual Creation* (Création artistique et création spirituelle) (Les Monts-de-Corsier, Switzerland: Prosveta Publishing, 1985).

[40] Sid Kirchheimer, "Mom's Voice Is Distinguished in Womb," *WebMD Medical News*, http://my.webmd.com/content/Article/64/72506.htm

[41] Alfred Tomatis, *The Uterine Night* (La nuit utérine) (Paris: Édition Stock, 1980).

[42] Ibid.

[43] See Psalm 139 of the King James Bible.

[44] Alfred Tomatis, *The Uterine Night* (La nuit utérine) (Paris: Édition Stock, 1980).

[45] Emile Osty, Bible de Jérusalem, traduction d'Emile Osty, éd. Seuil, Paris, 1973, www.omarlecheri.net/ency/daniel.htm

[46] Émile Coué, *Complete Works* (Oeuvres complètes) (Paris: Édition Astra, 1976).

[47] Karl Otto Schmidt, *Chance Does Not Exist* (Le hasard n'existe pas) (Paris: Édition Astra, 1956).

[48] Lama Anagarika Govinda, *Creative Meditation and Multidimensional Consciousness* (Méditation créatrice et conscience multidimentionnelle) (Paris: Albin Michel, 1979).

[49] Swami Bhaktivedanta, *Srimad-Bhagavatam.* (Los Angeles, CA: Bhaktivedanta Book Trust, 1991).

[50] Quoted in article by Michel Saint-Germain, *Resource Guide* 5:2 (November-December 1989).

[51] Ibid.

[52] George Balan, *În Dialog cu Emil Cioran* (Romania: Cartea Romãaneascæa, 1996).

[53] Isaac de Ninive, *Little Philocaly of the Prayer of the Heart* (Petite Philocalie de la prière du coeur) (Paris: Édition du Seuil, 1979).

[54] Bg. 7.8

[55] Swami Bhaktivedanta, *Vedanta Sutra* verse 1, chapter 17.

[56] Swami Bhaktivedanta, *Bhagavad Gita* (Paris: Bhaktivedanta Publishers, 1977).

[57] Bg. 8.13

[58] La Monte Young, *Selected Writings. The Chant of Pram Nath: The Sound is God* (Le Chant de Pram Nath: le son est Dieu) (Paris: Esselier, 1971).

[59] John Blofeld, *Mantras or the Power of Sacred Words* (Les mantras ou la puissance des mots sacrés) (Paris: Dervy-Livres, 1985).

[60] Deepak Chopra, *Quantum Healing: Exploring the Frontiers of Mind-Body Medicine* (New York, NY: Bantam, 1989).

[61] Cécile Beaudet and Richard Belfer, "Healing Music" (La musique qui soigne), *L'Impatient* 139 (June 1989).

[62] Ibid.

[63] Quoted in article by Michel Saint-Germain, *Resource Guide* 5:2 (November–December 1989).

[64] Hélène Caya, *From Sound Springs Light* (Du son jaillit la lumière) (Montreal: Denis J. Paradis Publishers, 1987).

[65] Marie-Louise Aucher, *Sonorous Man* (L'Homme sonore) (Paris: Epi, 1983).

[66] Isaac de Ninive, *Little Philocaly of the Prayer of the Heart* (Petite Philocalie de la prière du coeur) (Paris: Édition du Seuil, 1979).

[67] Bg. 9.27

[68] Jean During, *Music and Ecstasy* (Musique et extase) (Paris: Albin Michel, 1988).

[69] Bg. 8.20

[70] "Ista-deve Vijnapati" from Songs of the Vaisnava Acaryas, BBT 1974.

[71] Bg. 2.13.22

[72] Bg. 8.6

[73] Bg. 7.8

[74] Anne Osmont, in *Rhythm: Creator of Forces and Forms* (Le rythme: créateur de forces et de formes) (Paris: des Champs-Elysées, 1942).

GLOSSARY

ACHARYA: A spiritual master, often a lineage holder, who teaches through personal example.

ASHRAM: A residence or dwelling dedicated to the study, teaching and practice of spiritual life.

ATMA: The self; refers at different times to the body, senses or soul.

BHAGAVAD GITA: Hinduism's most popular wisdom book derived from the *Mahabharat.*

BHAJAN: Devotional songs, often sung in groups of devotees, directed toward divinity; may also refer to a state of fixed meditation.

BHAKTI: Love of God; devotion toward the Absolute.

BHAKTI YOGA: The system whereby pure devotional service to God is cultivated.

BIJA: The seed syllable or primary mantra.

BRAHMA: The creator-god of the Hindu deity triad.

BRAHMAN: The all-pervasive manifestation of Godhead.

BRAHMA-SAMHITA: An ancient text in which Brahma describes the form, the attributes and the realm of Absolute Truth, after the supreme being was revealed to him.

BUDDHI: The higher, intuitive mind; intelligence, awareness and wisdom.

CHAITANYA: The 15th Century Radha-Krishna avatar who began the bhakti yoga renaissance in Bengal by introducing congregational chanting of the Holy Names.

CHAKRA: Wheel, or disk. In Kundalini yoga, the center of consciousness or wheel of whirling energy (vortex-ring).

DEVA: Generally refers to one of the many deities of the Hindu pantheon.

DEVANAGARI: An alphabet descended from the Brahmi script originally developed to write Sanskrit.

GUNA: Threefold influence of material nature: *sattva*, *rajas* and *tamas*.

GURU: Spiritual teacher.

HARIDAS THAKUR: A disciple of Chaitanya Mahaprabhu who was given the title *namacharya*, master of the chanting of the Holy Names.

JAPA: Quiet chanting of the Holy Names normally performed with a *mala*, or prayer beads.

JIVA: The individual spirit soul or atomic living entity.

JIVA GOSWAMI: One of the six great sages of Vrindavan, the Indian village where Krishna performed his pastimes five thousand years ago.

KALI-YUGA: the present age of hypocrisy characterized by the progressive disappearance of spiritual principles in favor of the concern for material comfort. Lasting 432,000 years, it is the final age in a repeating cycle of four.

KIRTAN: Congregational chanting in glorification of God.

KRISHNA: "The one who attracts all beings toward Him." The original name of the supreme personality of Godhead.

MAHAMANTRA: The thirty-two-syllable mantra advocated by Chaitanya Mahaprabhu for deliverance in the age of Kali. This mantra not only holds the power to liberate conditioned beings from their material tendencies, it also awakens within them the divine love and ecstasy of inner life.

MANAS: The lower mind, which acts on behalf of the senses.

MANTRA: Sacred sound vibration that empowers the mind for concentration and transcendence of the ordinary.

MAYA: That which does not exist; the illusory energy.

NARADA MUNI: A son of Brahma; a great sage who travels everywhere spreading the glories of God by singing and playing his vina.

OMKARA: Or *om*; the spiritual sound vibration representing the Absolute.

PARAMATMA: The supersoul dwelling within the heart of all beings.

PARAMPARA: A spiritual lineage or succession of gurus.

PARA-PRAKRITI: *Prakriti:* nature (literally, what is directed).

PREMA: Pure love of God.

PURANA: A collection of eighteen Sanskrit texts dealing with the world's creation.

RAGA: In painting, the *ragas* describe an emotional moment provoked either by external agents (morning, evening, night, rain, storms, wind, etc.) or inner sentiments (sadness, love, longing, etc.). They combine with colors and lines to provoke an awakening of a certain number of emotions in the viewer. In music, it is the combination of modes and rhythms that must awaken diverse sensations and emotions in the listener.

RAMA: An inexhaustible source of felicity. Also designates the avatar Ramacandra.

RASA: Sacred aesthetic rapture in which the individual soul unites with God in a transcendental relationship.

RAVANA: The fiend who kidnaps Lord Rama's wife, Sita, in the Ramayana.

SADHANA: A spiritual discipline.

SANATAN DHARMA: The natural and eternal function of the soul, which is to create a link with the truth.

SRUTI: The revealed Vedic scriptures comprising the four Vedas, the Brahmanas and the Upanishads.

SUKADEV GOSWAMI: First orator of the *Srimad Bhagavatam.*

VEDA: Comprised of the Rig-Veda, Yajur-Veda, Sama-Veda and Atharva-Veda, which make up the Hindu canon.

YUGA: A cosmic age. There are four ages: *satya, treta, dvapara* and *kali.* A maha-yuga is one thousand cycles of the four ages, lasting 4,320,000 years, the duration of one day of Brahma.

BIBLIOGRaPHY

In preparing this publication, the author has primarily referenced French translations of books originally written in English. In such cases, both titles have been provided.

Achterberg, Jeanne. *Imagery in Healing.* Boston: Shambhala, 1985.

Aïvanhov, Omraam Mikhaël. *Artistic Creation and Spiritual Creation.* Les-Monts-de-Corsier, Switzerland: Provesta Publushing, 1985.

Aïvanhov, Omraam Mikhaël. *The Yoga of Nutrition.* Frejus, France: Provesta, 1982.

Alper, Dr. Frank. *Exploring Atlantis, Vols. 1-3.* Phoenix: Arizona Metaphysical Society, 1981.

Ashley-Farrand, Thomas. *Healing Mantras.* New York: The Ballantine Publishing Group, 1999.

Aucher, Marie-Louise. *Sonorous Man,* (L'Homme sonore). Paris: Epi, 1983.

Aurobindo, Sri. *The Synthesis of Yoga.* Pondicherry, India: Sri Aurobindo Ashram, 1976.

Bence, Léonce, and Max Méreaux. *Music for Healing* (La musique pour guérir). Unknown: Van de Velve, 1988.

Benenzon, Rolando. *Manual of Musicotherapy.* Unknown: Privat Publishers, 1981.

Berendt, Joachim-Ernst. *The World Is Sound: Nada Brahma.* Rochester, VT. Destiny Books, 1987.

Berg, Yehuda. *The 72 Names of God.* Los Angeles: The Kabbalah Centre, 2003.

Bertholet, Dr. Edward. *Reincarnation* (La Réincarnation). Unknown: Pierre Guenillard, 1978.

Besant, Annie. *The Power of Thought* (Le pouvoir de la pensée). Paris: Adyar, 1988.

Bhaktivedanta, Swami. *Chant and Be Happy*. Los Angeles: Bhaktivedanta Book Trust, 1982.

Bhaktivedanta, Swami. *Sri Namamrra*. Los Angeles: Bhaktivedanta Book Trust, 1982.

Blofeld, John. *Mantras or the Power of Sacred Words*. Unknown: Devry-Livres, 1985.

Bô-Yin-Râ. *The Practice of the Mantras* (La pratique des mantras). Paris: de Médicis Library, 1982.

Butor, M. *Words in Music* (Les mots dans la musique [Musique en jeu]). Unknown: du Seuil, 1971.

Campbell, Don. *The Mozart Effect*. New York: Avon Books, 1997.

Candé, Roland. *The Invitation to Music*. Roubaix, France: du Seuil, 1980.

Carton, Dr. Paul. *Treatise of Medicine, Nutrition and Natural Hygiene* (Traité de Médecine, d'alimentation et d'hygiène naturiste). Unknown: P. Carton, 1920.

Caya, Helene. *From Sound Springs Light* (Du son jaillit la lumiere). Montreal: Denis J. Paradis Inc. Publishers, 1987.

Chopra, Deepak. *Quantum Healing: Exploring the Frontiers of Mind-Body Medicine*. New York: Bantam, 1989.

Cotte, Roger J. V. *Music and Symbolism* (Musique et symbolisme). Saint-Jean de Braye, France: Dangles, 1988.

Das, Chaitanya Raghava. *The Divine Name*. Bombay: Sri Gaur Jayanti, 1954.

Diamond, Dr. John. *Your Body Doesn't Lie*. New York: Warner Books, 1980.

During, Jean. *Music and Ecstasy* (Musique et extase). Paris: Albin Michel Publishers, 1988.

Dossey, Larry, M.D. *Healing Words*. San Francisco: HarperSanFrancisco, 1993.

Eliade, Mircea. *Yoga: Immortality and Freedom*. Princeton, N.J.: Princeton University Press, 1973.

Emoto, Masaru. *Messages From Water Vol 2*. Tokyo, Japan: Hado Kyoikusha, 2001.

Feuerstein, Georg. *The Yoga Tradition*. Prescott, AZ.: Hohm Press, 1998.

Foglio, Hélène. *Sound Dynamics. Approach of the Sound Universe. Yoga, Sound and Prayer* (La dynamique du son. Approache de l'univers sonore. Yoga, son et prière). Paris: Courrier du livre, 1985.

Frédéric, Louis. *Dictionary of Indian Civilization* (Dictionnaire de la civilisation indienne). Montreal: Robert Laffont Publishers, 1987.

Garfield, Leah Maggie. *Sound Medicine.* Berkeley, CA: Celestial Arts, 1987.

Gass, Robert. *Chanting.* New York: Broadway Books/Random House, 1999.

Gaynor, Mitchelf. *The Healing Power of Sound.* Boston: Shambhala Publications, 2002.

Goswami, Amit. *The Self-Aware Universe: How Consciousness Creates the Material World.* New York: Tarcher/Putman, 1993.

Goswami, Rupa. *The Nectar of Devotion,* tr. Swami Bhaktivedanta. Los Angeles, CA: Bhaktivedanta Book Trust, 1970.

Gregorat, Claudio. *Music's Spiritual Experience* (L'expérience spirituelle de la musique). Paris: Centre Triades Publishers, 1980.

Guillot, J. and M. A., J. Jost, and E. Lecourt. *Musicotherapy and New Methods of Associating Techniques* (La Musicothérapie et les méthodes nouvelles d'association des techniques). Paris: EST, 1977.

Hall, Manly P. *The Therapeutic Value of Music Including the Philosophy of Music.* Los Angeles, CA: Philosophical Research Society, 1982.

Hamel, Peter Michael. *Through Music to the Self.* New York, NY: Element Books, 1978.

Hanish, Dr. A. *Course in Harmony* (Cours d'harmonie). Paris: Aryana, 1967.

Harner, Michael. *The Way of the Shaman.* San Francisco, CA: HarperSanFrancisco: 1990.

Heline, Corinne. *Color and Music in the New Age.* Los Angeles, CA: New Age Press Inc, 1964.

Heline, Corinne. *The Cosmic Harp.* Santa Monica, CA.: New Age Bible and Philosophy Center, 1986.

Huneau, Sophie. *Healing Musics* (Les musiques qui guérissent). Paris: Retz, 1985.

Howard, W. *The Music and the Child* (La musique et l'enfant). Paris: PUF, 1963.

Khan, Hazrat Inayat. *The Music of Life.* New Lebanon: Omega Publications, 1988.

Khan, Sufi Inayat. *Music.* Lahore, Pakistan: Sh. Muhammad Ashraf, 1971.

Kuhne, Louis. *The New Science of Healing* (La Nouvelle Science de guérir). Paris: Cevic, 1978.

Kushi, Aveline and Michio. *Macrobiotic Pregnancy and Care of the Newborn.* Paris: Guy Tredaniel Publishers, 1986.

Lachat, Jean. *Musicotherapy* (Musicothérapie). Montreal: Guérin, 1981.

Laskow, Leonard. *Healing with Love.* San Francisco, CA: HarperSanFrancisco, 1992.

Leeds, Joshua. *The Power of Sound.* Rochester, VT: Healing Arts Press, 2001.

Lingerman, Hal A. *The Healing Energies of Music.* Wheaton, IL: The Theosophical Publishing House, 1983.

Maltz, Maswell. *Psycho-Cybernetics.* Los Angeles, CA: Wilshire Books, 1968.

Marshall, Henry. *Mantras.* Amsterdam: Bluestar Communications, 1999.

McCellan, Randolf. *The Healing Forces of Music.* New York, NY; Amity House, 1988.

Menuhin, Yehudi, and Curtis W. Davis. *The Music of Man.* Unknown: Olympic Marketing Corp., 1979.

Michell, John. *The Dimensions of Paradise.* San Francisco, CA: Harper & Row, 1988.

Montello, Louise. *Essential Musical Intelligence.* Wheaton, IL: The Theosophical Publishing House, 2002.

Mumford, John. *Psychosomatic Yoga.* London: Thorsons, 1962.

Podolsky, E. *The Doctor Prescribes Music.* New York, NY: Frederick A. Stockes Co., 1939.

Puri, Swami B.P. *Art of Sadhana.* San Francisco: Mandala Publishing, 1999.

Quertant, G. *Music and Medicine* (Musique et médecine). Unknown: Unknown, 1933.

Reeves, Hubert. *Time for Elation. Does the universe have a meaning?* (Le temps de s'enivrer. L'Univers a-t'il un sens?). Roubaix, France: du Seuil, 1985.

Rudhyar, Dane. *The Magic of Tone and the Art of Music.* Unknown: Arista Publishers, 1985.

Schullian, D. M. and M. Schoen. *Music and Medicine.* New York, NY: Schumann, 1948.

Scott, Cyril. *Music: Its Secret Influence Through the Ages.* Unknown: de la Baconniere Publishers, 1984.

Sivananda, Sri Swami. *Japa Yoga.* Montreal: Sivananda International Centre of Vedanta Yoga, 1956.

Sivananda, Sri Swami. *Music as Yoga.* Rishikesh, India: Yoga-Vedanta Forest University, 1956.

Sridhar, Swami B.R. *Subjective Evolution of Consciousness: The Play of the Sweet Absolute.* San Jose, CA: Guardian of Devotion Press, 1989.

Stevens, S. S., and Fred Varshofsky. *Sound and Listening.* New York, NY: Time, 1966.

Tame, David. *The Secret Power of Music.* Rochester, VT:Destiny Books, 1989.

Tegtmeier, Ralph. *Guide to New Musics.* Unknown: Le Souffle d'Or Publishers, 1988.

Teplov, B. M. *Psychology of Musical Aptitudes* (Psychologie des aptitudes musicales). Paris: PUF, 1966.

Tomatis, Alfred. *The Ear and Language* (L'Oreille et le langage). Roubaix, France: du Seuil, 1978.

Tomatis, Alfred. *The Ear and Life* (L'Oreille et la vie). Roubaix, France: du Seuil, 1978.

Tompkins, Peter, and Christopher Bird. *The Secret Life of Plants* (La vie secrète des plantes). Montreal: Robert Laffont, 1973.

Tripurari, Swami B.V. *The Bhagavad Gita: Its Feeling and Philosophy.* San Rafael, CA: Mandala Publishing, 2001.

Vajpeyi, Kailash. *The Science of Mantras* (La science des mantras). Paris: Guy Trédaniel, 1977.

Weber, Edith. *Musicological Research* (La recherche musicologique). Paris: Beauchesne, 1980.

Wilber, Ken, ed. *Quantum Question: The Mystical Writings of the World's Great Physicists.* Boston: Shambhala, 1984.

Young, La Monte. *Selected Writings. The Chant of Pram Nath: The Sound is God* (Le chant de pram nath: le son est Dieu). Paris: Esselier, 1971.

AUTHOR'S REQUEST

I would appreciate hearing from readers and listeners of my recording material. My research in healing
music continues and I am especially interested in
listeners who are touched, transformed, healed, or encounter a life-changing experience after listening to
one of my recordings or live concerts. Please write to
the following address:

info@patrickbernard.com
or
Music as Yoga Resource Center
C.P. 183 Ste-Agathe-des-Monts
Quebec, J8C 3A2
Canada

Thank you.

PATRICK BERNARD
complete discography

TITLE	ITEM #	PRICE (U.S.)
Atlantis Angelis	MAGHCD88	$16.95
Solaris Universalis	MAGHCD89	$16.95
Shamanyka	MAGHCD90	$16.95
Mantra Rock Project	MAGHCD91	$16.95
Image Voyage	MAGHCD93	$16.95
Amor Immortalis	MAGHCD92	$16.95
Mantra Mandala	MAGHCD82	$16.95
Manuscript Du Silence	MAGHCD84	$16.95
Atlantis Angelis II	MAGHCD121	$16.95
Sublime Relaxation	MAGCD116	$16.95
Love Divine	MAGCD126	$16.95
Supreme Moment	MAGCD133	$18.95

To order CDs, please visit www.patrickbernard.com

OTHER TITLES AVAILABLE *through* MANDALA PUBLISHING

$19.95 US

SMARANAM
A Garland of Kirtan

AUTHOR: James Bae
ARTIST: Agni Deva
GUEST INSTRUMENTALIST:
Hans Christian of Rasa

Hardbound CD-Book / 78 pp, 66 min.
5.25 " x 5.5 ", 5-color / 26 illustrations
ISBN: 1-886069-49-2, $19.95 US

KIRTAN
Chanting the Names

AUTHOR: Swami B.B. Bodhayan
ARTIST: Agni Deva
GUEST INSTRUMENTALIST:
Hans Christian of Rasa

$19.95 US

Hardbound CD-Book / 88 pp, 66 min.
5.25 " x 5.5 ", 5-color / 59 illustrations
ISBN: 1-886069-78-6

To order, please call 800.688.2218 or visit www.mandala.org